TABLES FROM THE RUBBLE

HOW THE RESTAURANTS THAT AROSE AFTER THE GREAT QUAKE STILL FEED SAN FRANCISCO TODAY

Denise E. Clifton

Tandemvines Media
Seattle, Washington

Tandemvines Media
505 Broadway E., No. 283
Seattle, Wash. 98102
www.tandemvines.com

A multimedia edition iBook of *Tables From The Rubble* was published in 2012 and updated in 2017. See more about the iBook at www.tandemvines.com.

Both the 2012 and 2017 editions contain some material previously published as a freelance article Feb. 26, 2012, in the *Seattle Times*, with rights reserved by Denise Clifton.

Photograph permissions credits appear with each image. Photos in this book have been provided for use with permission by the California State Library, Sacramento, California; California Historical Society; The Bancroft Library, University of California, Berkeley; Chinese Historical Society of America; Library of Congress; San Francisco History Center, San Francisco Public Library; U.S. Geological Survey; Geri Migielicz of Story4; Christopher Cellars and Denise Clifton of Tandemvines Media; and several restaurants in San Francisco, California.

The cover image shows one of the last "ham and egg shacks" in downtown San Francisco in 1907, and is courtesy of the California History Room, California State Library.

Book design Tandemvines Media

ISBN: 978-0-9882747-1-6

CONTENTS

For the families who generously share their stories and their tables

A NOTE FROM THE AUTHOR

I N A CITY where rotting Gold Rush-era ships are still unearthed when glittering new skyscrapers are built, new pieces of the San Francisco story are always coming to the surface. A trove of old photos is found in an archive. Dusty documents become digitized and searchable. A century-old restaurant loses one home and finds another, and a bartender tells an old story to a new person.

In the years since I started telling the tales of *Tables From The Rubble*, which was first published as a multimedia iBook in 2012 and updated in 2017, I've learned that this is not a book that simply ends. Rather, it's been a beginning – a collection of stories that continue to build on each other as new layers are revealed.

In this edition, we learn about the La Rocca family's "Crab King," who started out selling crabs from a wheelbarrow and built a seafood distribution business that is still supplying Bay Area chefs 110 years later. We visit the Comstock Saloon and glimpse its earliest days, when boxers worked the door and fights were "settled" at the bar. We tuck into a lamb-chop lunch at John's Grill, which has a cinematic past and a power-broker present, and tip back a pint at Schroeder's, where the murals on the walls were painted in exchange for food and drink.

We've also learned of some new twists in catching up with our old favorites. All are still going strong. Best of all, the Sam Wo story – which was a cliffhanger when *Tables From The Rubble* first published – has a happy ending. After three and a half years of hard work, the efforts of the community and the Ho family paid off. The tiny restaurant, beloved for its cheap traditional food and famous for once having the "world's rudest waiter," reopened to fanfare and a lion dance in October 2015.

I'm forever grateful to these hard-working families and owners who share their stories at their own tables. Together they offer a richer look into a century of culinary experiences that still shape San Francisco.

The joy comes from savoring the journey. Thanks for coming with me.

Denise Clifton, Fall 2017

THE CITY THAT IS

Refugees dine at a temporary restaurant set up among San Francisco's ruins.
(California Historical Society, FN - 26857)

"Many of the street lunch counters in a spirit of fun, affected the high-sounding names of fashionable restaurants that had gone down in the general wreck, such as the Poodle Dog, Marchand's, Delmonico ... Others were more original, posting such signs as, 'Earthquake shakes, 5c. a glass' ... The inscription that afforded most amusement perhaps, was the one saying: 'Eat, drink and be merry, for tomorrow we may have to go to Oakland.'"

– Sunset magazine, October 1906

The west side of Nob Hill neighborhood soon after the earthquake, as seen from the corner of Van Ness Avenue and Washington Street. (U.S. Geological Survey)

AT THE BEGINNING OF THE TWENTIETH CENTURY, San Francisco wanted nothing more than to be known as the "Paris of the West." The city was celebrated by residents and visitors from around the world for its many cosmopolitan delights – including its restaurants – and one of the early favorite dining establishments, the Old Poodle Dog, had just marked its fiftieth anniversary. The city was home to more than 400,000 residents, including railroad tycoons who lived in palatial Nob Hill mansions and favored French-style fine restaurants, and transient laborers who worked the wharf and grabbed their dinners at cheap cafes that dotted the city.

On April 18, 1906, the city's dreams were crushed. The powerful 7.9 earthquake and the three days of fires that followed didn't discriminate between the classes: Residents of mansions and flophouses fled their homes for the city's parks, and the finest restaurants joined the lowliest cafes in rubble that was several feet deep in places and spread for miles.

Impromptu kitchens immediately sprang up in the streets as indoor cooking was prohibited citywide. Fallen bricks were often used for fireplaces – and overturned sinks sometimes became stovetops. Dozens of photographs survive to show women in heavy long dresses bending over stoves set on curbs, and men in suits and derby hats eating standing up or gathered around makeshift tables.

Refugees cook near a camp at Market and Buchanan streets.
(Bear Photo Co., California History Room, California State Library)

As news of the devastation reached the East Coast, San Francisco was quickly written off. On April 21, *The (New York) Sun* published an essay titled *The City That Was* that opened with the proclamation, "The old San Francisco is dead." Restaurants were among the many losses lamented in the piece written by Will Irwin, a journalist who had once lived and worked in the Bay Area:

"It was noted for its restaurants. Perhaps the very best, for people who do not care how they spend their money, could not be had there, but for a dollar, 75 cents, 50 cents, a quarter, or even fifteen cents, the restaurants afforded the best fare on earth for the price. ... The country all about produced everything that a cook needs and that in abundance – the bay was an almost untapped fishing pound [sic], the fruit farms came up to the very edge of the town, and the surrounding country produced in abundance fine meats, all cereals and all vegetables. ... Householders always dined out one or two nights of the week, and boarding houses were scarce, for the unattached preferred the restaurants. The eating was usually better than the surroundings. Meals that were marvels were served in tumbledown little hotels."

– The (New York) Sun, April 21, 1906

The essay was later expanded into a small book, *The City That Was: A Requiem for Old San Francisco*, and in that version, waxing even more nostalgic, Irwin added this closing statement: "The bonny, merry city – the good, gray city – O that one who has mingled the wine of her bounding life with the wine of his youth should live to write the obituary of Old San Francisco!" The 47-page book sold so well nationally that it was reprinted at least four times.

San Francisco editors and business leaders were unhappy to be dismissed so quickly by the East Coast press. Yes, more than four square miles of buildings were flattened and scorched, the water supply was compromised and hundreds of thousands of residents were camped out in parks or huddled across the bay in Oakland, but local newspapers were already spinning positive.

On the same day that the city was declared dead by *The Sun*, the *San Francisco Call's* top headline was dire: "WATER FRONT BURNS ALMOST TO THE FERRY." But underneath it, another headline proclaimed, "WILL RISE AGAIN IN SPLENDOR." The paper wrote, "The spirit of the hour is that the city will rise again in renewed splendor and in such form that the dream of beautiful San Francisco will be realized."

One of the last "ham and egg shacks" in 1907. These street kitchens were the only available restaurants downtown right after the fires. (California History Room, California State Library)

The residents quickly got to work. Within about a week, a little electricity had been restored, a few streetcars were running on Market Street, and the newspapers were full of breathless rebuilding news. Reports of death and devastation were downplayed, pushed to pages far inside or out of the newspapers altogether.

During the weeks after the disaster, restaurants became vital to the recovery effort because they were a key part of food distribution. In May 1906, leaders of the Red Cross urged that restaurants be allowed to open quickly to help feed the refugees camping out across the city. Dr. Edward Levine, who led the Red Cross's initial relief efforts, wrote:

"I would recommend … that the speedy opening of restaurants where cooked meals can be purchased at a price not to exceed fifteen cents be encouraged and facilitated by the sale to responsible persons of surplus stores of certain kinds now in the hands of the Commissary."

A sign brags of the luxuries a restaurant has for sale in the shadow of the damaged City Hall dome. (California Historical Society, FN - 34566)

Fior d'Italia, an Italian restaurant that had already been open for more than 30 years in the North Beach neighborhood, was one of the restaurants that set up a kitchen in a tent right away to feed soup to people forced to camp in nearby Washington Square park. Fior continued to operate out of a tent for at least a year after the quake.

Restaurants and street kitchens were also primary social centers and sources for information – and neighborly help – for the suddenly homeless population, some of whom had to live in refugee camps in places like Golden Gate Park or the Presidio for more than two years.

One enterprising refugee, recognizing that many women's cookbooks had been lost in the disaster, published *The Refugees' Cook Book,* which offered fifty recipes for fifty cents. Fourteen "patronesses" underwrote the printing.

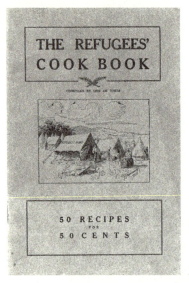

How to make "Chippine"

San Francisco's Italian fishermen living in North Beach had made cioppino a favorite local dish by the turn of the twentieth century. The stew traditionally included fish and shellfish simmered with tomatoes and wine, and the name comes from a Genoese word for "little soup." After the quake, a recipe for "chippine" was among several seafood recipes that made it into *The Refugees' Cook Book:*

"Take a good-sized solid piece of fish (bass or white fish) put in a pot with one can of tomatoes, one onion sauted (sic) in butter, two pepper pods, one bay leaf, juice of one dozen clams, cook briskly one hour; fifteen minutes before serving add one dozen clam bellies."

In addition to recipes for soups, salads, entrees, and ice cream, the writer offered tips for filtering water, and "to clear your house or tent of flies," she encouraged readers to burn cayenne pepper in a pan and open a window.

By fall 1906, with rebuilding efforts in full swing, *Sunset* magazine published one of its many indignant responses to *The Sun* obituary. The magazine pointed out that restaurants were among the first businesses to start to recover. They might have been operating in tents like Fior or in flimsy shacks – indoor cooking continued to be banned for months in some neighborhoods as the city struggled to contain the fire danger – but they were open, nonetheless.

"On Fillmore Street, in little dinky quarters, on Van Ness Avenue among former private residences and elsewhere in the unharmed districts of the city, such restaurants as Delmonico's, Tait's, Techau's

and the Poodle Dog reappeared. Meanwhile in the Latin quarter the old Bohemian haunts such as Matias' Mexican fonda, or the Buon Gusto, Fior d'Italia, and others of their ilk sprang to life again in little wooden shacks arising from the ruins of their former establishments. It was like the clusters of wild lilies and nasturtium that here and there have sprung from the ruins of former gardens in San Francisco, flecking the dismal ashes with gleams of color and fragrance."

– Rufus Steele, Sunset magazine, October 1906

One year after the earthquake, a restaurant made of boxes sits on school property at Market and Fifth streets. (California History Room, California State Library)

More dining and drinking establishments came back as the city did, sometimes operating in half-completed structures for years. About 28,000 buildings had been destroyed in the quake. City politics were chaotic – within months, Mayor Eugene Schmitz's administration was on trial for graft – and some of the initial plans to require buildings to be more quake- and fire-resistant were scrapped in the rush to rebuild. Construction permits were granted fast and furiously – more than 6,000 by June 1907 – but building was often delayed because materials and manpower were in short supply. There was so much work that for a time it was said that laborers and carpenters could set their own wages for overtime.

This map commissioned by the California Promotions Committee shows the buildings under construction two years after the earthquake. (Library of Congress)

Some areas like North Beach, which was close to the wharf where the supplies came in, recovered relatively quickly. Just a few blocks down the hill, Chinatown had to fight to rebuild at all, fending off an effort by city powers to relocate the neighborhood far from downtown.

In spring 1909, on the third anniversary of the quake, *Sunset* published a story to extol San Francisco's recovery. In direct response to Will Irwin's "requiem," it was titled *The City That Is*, and in October 1909, it, too, became a small book. In the piece, writer Rufus Steele assesses the state of San Francisco's restaurants:

> *"The restaurants are as good as they were and as bad as they were,*
> *no less cosmopolitan and distinctive, and the patrons who loved their*

life – who made their life – still eat, drink and smoke around the
board. There is lacking only the cobwebs in the cellar, a fault which
time will right."

– The City That Is, Rufus Steele, October 1909

By that fall, in time for San Francisco's five-day Portolá Festival, much of the cityscape was rebuilt or well into the process of rebuilding. Six years later, when 18 million people attended the Panama-Pacific International Exposition in 1915, San Francisco celebrated its complete reconstruction on a world stage.

During these heady boom years, when new buildings rose on top of charred debris as fast as lumber arrived from the Pacific Northwest, many restaurateurs and other business owners who had seen their establishments reduced to rubble found a way to revive and thrive.

Other entrepreneurs opened their cafes for the first time, finding opportunity in the hunger of a city that was growing again. A few hundred restaurants were listed in city directories by 1908; by 1915 the number had doubled.

A century later, most of the restaurants that rose from the ruins have since fallen victim to economic woes or changes in tastes. Delmonico disappears from directories around 1920. The celebrated Old Poodle Dog was reincarnated a number of times during the twentieth century before closing for good in the mid-1980s.

Fior d'Italia moved many times in the North Beach neighborhood and stayed open for another 100-plus years before closing in May 2012.

Tadich Grill is still around and claims the title of California's oldest restaurant, but it has been forced to relocate several times in the decades since the earthquake, holding onto a celebrated name and long history, though in a more modern setting.

But tucked around the city, I discovered a handful of original survivors – restaurants where I joined customers savoring good food straight out of century-old menus, served up in some of the same spaces that opened in the heady years after the earthquake.

Swan Oyster Depot on Polk Street opened in 1912. (Tandemvines Media, 2012)

Slurping down briny oysters at Swan Oyster Depot on Polk Street, I rested my elbows on the marble counter that customers have been flocking to since 1912.

I waited in line at Liguria Bakery in North Beach like the locals have since 1911, and took my warm focaccia studded with garlic and rosemary across the street to eat in Washington Square park.

I bellied up to the bar for a pre-Prohibition-style cocktail at the Comstock Saloon, where boxers worked as bouncers and fights were "settled" in the years right after the quake, when it was known as Jim Griffin's Andromeda Saloon.

Down the hill in Chinatown, I walked through the narrow kitchen and up creaking stairs to enjoy handmade rice noodles at tiny Sam Wo on Washington Street, and then stood in line with customers who waited hours for one more meal when the city closed the 104-year-old restaurant down. It took three and a half years of sweat and tears – and the tenacious will of a large community and a small family – but in 2015 Sam Wo reopened a couple of blocks away.

David Ho in Sam Wo's original main-floor kitchen on Washington Street.
(Tandemvines Media, 2012)

There were hearty Sam Spade's lamb chops at John's Grill (catering to politicians, executives – and even writers – since 1908), and frothy German beers and housemade brats at Schroeder's, whose first owner was an early champion of the recovering downtown.

Sitting in splendor under the grand glass ceiling at the Garden Court in the Palace Hotel, I reveled in fresh crab salad, on the menu since the reopening in 1909.

And then I crossed the street to sip a beer in the afternoon at the House of Shields, where the bar has been serving men since 1912 – and women, too, since 1972.

These are among the handful of establishments that remain in San Francisco from the post-earthquake boom years, offering food, drinks, and stories with direct links to a century-old past. Together, these places capture the flavors of a city that was piecing itself back together and still reaching for greatness – with recent immigrants and wealthy families alike starting over to make a living in a place known for its food.

Step through their doors for a bite of lunch, a late-night snack, a cocktail – and enjoy a taste of this resilient time period. As Rufus Steele wrote for *Sunset* in 1909, "the 'old San Francisco' is very much alive."

THE VIEW FROM GEORGE LAWRENCE'S "CAPTIVE AIRSHIP"

The view of the devastated city in May 1906, from George R. Lawrence's "Captive Airship." The ferry building can be seen standing at the foot of Market Street, just left of center. (Library of Congress)

GEORGE R. LAWRENCE was a commercial photographer in turn-of-the-century Chicago who was famous for building his own large-format cameras and experimenting with aerial photography using hot-air balloons. In 1900, he was awarded the "Grand Prize of the World for Excellence in Photography" at the Paris Exposition for building a 1,400-pound camera to photograph a new train. His company's slogan was "The Hitherto Impossible in Photography is Our Specialty."

By 1906 he had created an apparatus he called the "Captive Airship," based on kites that were originally invented to carry banner advertising. Lawrence adapted the advertising kites, creating a train of five to seventeen kites and using them to hoist giant cameras he built from wood and aluminum. (The number of kites in the train depended on the size of the camera he was using.) A system of booms, lead weights and lines stabilized the cameras, and Lawrence used an electrical current carried through an insulated wire to trigger the shutter from the ground.

With the Captive Airship, Lawrence could take photographs from 2,000 feet in the air, long before aerial photography from airplanes became common. When he heard the news of the devastation in San Francisco, Lawrence saw an opportunity to show what his Captive Airship could do.

Within a few weeks, he was flying his kite trains from several points high above the ruins, capturing sharp panoramic images with homemade cameras that weighed 49 pounds and held film plates measuring 48 inches by 20 inches. Those who've seen the original enormous contact prints say they can clearly see people standing in San Francisco's rubble, looking up at the Captive Airship in the sky. Lawrence was able to sell single prints for $125 apiece and reportedly earned about $15,000 in his lifetime for his pictures of the San Francisco disaster.

– *Source: Simon Baker, "San Francisco in Ruins: The 1906 Aerial Photographs of George R. Lawrence," Landscape, Vol. 30, No. 2, 1989, 9-14*

TWO BANDS OF BROTHERS

This 1922 photo shows that in its early years, Swan Oyster Depot was about twice as wide as it is today. (Sancimino family)

"Change should be like breeze in a cathedral. You want enough to keep it fresh, but not enough to blow out the candles."

– Jimmy Sancimino

Swan Oyster Depot's front window shows off what's fresh and available each day. Steve Sancimino, left, works with his nephew Erik Wideman to put together a salad order. Erik started working at Swan when he was 15. (Tandemvines Media, 2011)

TUCK IN TIGHT ON A STOOL between the locals and tourists, slurp through a dozen (or two) Tomales Bay oysters, and consider: For more than 100 years, Swan Oyster Depot has been serving up the same menu, at the same marble counter, in the same narrow shop on Polk Street.

It may look plain, but Swan qualifies as San Francisco dining royalty, landing on best-restaurant lists like Zagat's and Eater's every year. The counter is a regular stop for celebrities like chef/author/raconteur Anthony Bourdain. But this isn't a place that take its cues from ratings. Swan emerged from the ashes after the earthquake, stuck with one simple plan – fresh seafood, no fuss – and became a legend.

In 1907, Western Nob Hill is completely under reconstruction, as cable cars run this stretch of California Street from Leavenworth toward Van Ness. Swan would open a few years later on Polk Street, in the block east of Van Ness and north of California. (California History Room, California State Library)

Swan Oyster Depot has been owned by just two families since it opened in 1912. Before the quake, a Danish family named Lausten had owned an oyster shop on the west slope of Nob Hill that was destroyed in the fires. Afterward, according to the *San Francisco Chronicle*, one of the Lausten brothers drove a wagon to Oakland, bought provisions, and returned to Golden Gate Park to give them away to city residents under a sign that read: "Free flour and water from Swan Oyster Depot. Remember us."

Photographs from 1906 show desolate streets with gnarled, burned-out cable cars lying along the west end of the California Street line, around the corner from where Swan is today. The fires had been held back the next block over, on Van Ness Avenue, and many businesses from around the city were temporarily relocated to that street during the rebuilding period. Within a year, the Nob Hill neighborhood was well into reconstruction, and a shopping district soon bustled again along Polk Street.

Three years after the quake – at a time when the city was promoting its recovery – oysters were such a part of its culinary experience that the *San Francisco Call* specifically celebrated the return of the oyster shops: "San Francisco's oyster houses were famous before the fire. They were cozy retreats with an atmosphere of quaint hospitality not to be found elsewhere and they made a specialty of supplying the most luscious oysters to be bought in the market. ... These establishments did not perish with the fire of three years ago. It is true that some of them have sought new locations, but nearly all of them are in business again and are serving oysters of the same high quality as before."

It was 1912 when the Laustens opened Swan Oyster Depot at 1517 Polk St. Records indicate that three or four of the Lausten brothers ran the shop and that the space was shared with a market. A photo from 1922 shows that the original space was about twice the width of the current cafe, which still has the original floor.

Around 1936 a wall was put in, making Swan's space narrower and allowing the business to share space with another shop next door. Until 2009, this spot housed a See's Candies, one of the few standalone shops in that chain.

When the Danes were ready to retire in 1946, Sal Sancimino partnered with cousins in the La Rocca family, who had been distributing seafood in the city since before the quake, to buy the shop. Sal had grown up in North Beach and many in his extended family worked on fishing boats, but Sal had a "bum ear" that caused him to get seasick. The oyster shop was a way to stay in the seafood business without going to sea.

Five of Sal's sons still run Swan Oyster Depot today, and all started working there as kids. One of the youngest, Jimmy Sancimino, remembers standing on a milk crate to wash dishes and riding shotgun on the delivery trucks. By the time he was in sixth grade, he and his brothers were working in the shop pretty much full time in the summers. "It was good," he said. "It taught us that work is good, work is fun." He said kids in the big Sancimino family still start out this way. "Like the old-fashioned tradesmen, we start as apprentices."

In 1957, Sal Sancimino, left, and Frank Farone get the counter ready for customers. Sal bought Swan in 1946 and owned it until he died in 1989; Frank would work at Swan for around 20 years. (Sancimino family)

It wasn't always a given that the Sancimino brothers would end up working at Swan. Jimmy said most of them tried other careers in their early working lives – one was a lawyer for a while – but they kept coming back to the oyster shop. "Nothing else was as fun."

Plus, he said, sweeping his hand above the window stuffed with fresh fish and shellfish, "We get to eat better than 99 percent of the world."

Swan still gets seafood from the La Roccas, and many members of the Sanciminos' extended family and friends work the busy counter. Menus in the black-and-white photos covering the walls look nearly identical to the one posted above the counter: oysters, bay shrimp, prawns, crab in season. All fresh, offered with lemon, mignonette, cocktail sauce, bread and butter.

"Change should be like breeze in a cathedral," Jimmy said. "You want enough to keep it fresh, but not enough to blow out the candles."

Jimmy Sancimino, left, works the same counter his father did. Customers start lining up outside on Polk Street well before Swan Oyster Depot opens at 10:30 a.m.
(Tandemvines Media, 2011)

His dad added clam chowder, salads, and beer and wine in the early 1960s, and Swan still uses Sal's chowder recipe. Smoked fish, crayfish, and lobster are available to eat in or take out, and fresh fish can be bought to cook at home. Some San Francisco families have been eating at Swan for six generations, and those in the know will ask for items that aren't listed on the menu – a plate of crab legs, for example.

The brothers say that the options for seafood haven't changed much – although the ever-popular Olympia oysters are now harder to come by, and turtles are no longer legally available in California for the turtle soup that was a favorite among early twentieth-century Pacific Heights millionaires' wives and their personal chefs. As it has since 1912, Swan still delivers seafood to houses around town – but fortunately the days of negotiating the city's hills by horse and wagon are long over.

Early in the mornings, the Sanciminos and their crew cut fish and prep orders for the day. By the time they open the counter at 10:30 a.m., more than a dozen hungry customers are already lined up to snag one of the 18 stools. Regulars are greeted with cheers – and a beer if they have to wait for a takeout order.

On a stool toward the back, Kathryn Szydlowski, who worked as a printer at the *San Francisco Chronicle* for decades, said she and her friends started coming to Swan in 1973, and she always stops in when she's in the neighborhood. "I've known these guys since they were kids," she said, waving at two of the Sancimino brothers behind the counter.

Steve Sancimino, Jimmy's older brother, sees similarities between the tumultuous times when the Laustens opened Swan after the earthquake and when his dad took it over in the mid-1940s: "After 1906, there was an incredible renaissance of building in San Francisco. Likewise, after the war." Both time periods forced families to move and businesses to close or change hands.

All these years later, Steve shrugs and smiles while cutting up sole when asked about a Zagat rating. (Swan Oyster Depot was also named the best seafood restaurant in Zagat's first Bay Area survey in 1987.) He credits the success to his family's commitment: "One of us is here every day." And it helps that the brothers share the workload and have a good time doing it. "We have a zest for life and a zest for work."

1517 Polk St.
415-673-1101
No website.
Open Monday-Saturday, 10:30 a.m. to 5 p.m. Each year the shop closes around the Fourth of July so the Sanciminos can take a family vacation. Sometimes the counter also closes for a few days around Christmas because of the holiday rush.

SAL SANCIMINO'S CLAM CHOWDER

(Christopher Cellars, 2011)

Ingredients:

- 1/4 cup butter
- 1/2 white onion, chopped
- 1 pint fresh shucked raw clams, chopped
- 1 large russet potato, cubed in 1/2-inch pieces, parboiled (boiled for about 15 minutes)
- 1 pint whole milk
- 1 pint half-and-half

Directions: Sauté onion in butter until clear. Add milk, half-and-half, potato and clams. Heat slowly (on low) in double boiler. Stir frequently; salt and pepper to taste.

Note: The pot you cook the chowder in must be placed in a slightly larger pot or double boiler with water in it. This is to prevent the chowder from burning and to reduce the risk of the milk separating. Cooking it on low and stirring frequently will also reduce the risk of separation.

Serve with French bread and butter. Makes 4-6 servings.

- Recipe courtesy of the Sancimino family

"NATIVE OYSTERS ARE SMALL, BUT SWEET"

San Francisco Call, April 20, 1909

On the third anniversary of the quake, the city's institutions enthusiastically touted its recovery. At the time, the local oyster fishery was still one of the top industries for the area. This is an excerpt from one of the San Francisco Call stories promoting the city's cuisine:

"THE OYSTER OF SAN FRANCISCO IS FAMOUS. Its celebrity has gone forth to the ends of the earth, carried by the eloquent tongues of the gourmand, native or visitor, who has tasted, smacked his lips, tasted again, and instantly has become the willing slave to the appetite for the delicious bivalve that thrives upon the oyster beds of San Francisco bay.

San Francisco bay is an extensive sheet of water. It includes not only the water front known by the commuter, but long miles more in every direction, some parts known by other names, and some reaches rarely visited by the ordinary city dweller. Along its great extent of shores the oyster lies contentedly in his muddy couch, fattening for the epicure.

There are, generally speaking, two classes of oysters for sale in the cafes, restaurants, oyster grottoes and retail stores of this city. There are the so called California oysters. This is the real Pacific coast oyster. He is an aborigine, he belongs to the soil and his father and grandfather and great-grandfather oysters dwelt before him in the same ooze which he finds so satisfactory as a place of residence. This oyster is small but very, very delicious. What he lacks in size he more than makes up in palatable sweetness. San Francisco and California are proud of him and to show that pride, consume him in enormous quantities.

Then there is the eastern oyster. The eastern oyster does not belong here, as his name indicates, he is a stranger in our midst, an unwilling visitor, never consulted before he was unceremoniously torn from his old home and the association of his dear family and friends in Chesapeake bay and other places on the Atlantic coast. In other words, this is the transplanted oyster. Brought to this coast when very small, the eastern oysters are placed in oyster beds which have been found suitable for their growth. They grow to fine size and rival the delicacy and appetizing quality of the native son oyster. And so it is that the San Franciscan may have upon his table at home or in the restaurant the toke point, the blue point, or any other variety which he most affects.

The retail oyster business is also a very profitable one. It flourishes in every section of the city, for San Francisco is undeniably an oyster eating community, and it takes many dealers to supply the big demand from day to day.

San Francisco's oyster houses were famous before the fire. They were cozy retreats with an atmosphere of quaint hospitality not to be found elsewhere and they made a specialty of supplying the most luscious oysters to be bought in the market. Many of them had their regular patrons, men and women who had been coming year after year to indulge their taste for the enchanting bivalve.

These establishments did not perish with the fire of three years ago. It is true that some of them have sought new locations, but nearly all of them are in business again and are serving oysters of the same high quality as before. A number are to be found in the old locations and the old patrons who return to them will have the pleasure of satisfying their taste for oysters and at the same time meditating on the old days before the fire.

It would take the pen of a poet guided by the imagination of an epicure to do any sort of justice to the oysters of San Francisco. They are a joy forever, an emblem of good fellowship, the forerunner of delicately prepared meals, and they are never so enjoyable as when they are consumed to the accompaniment of a pint of any of San Francisco's famous brews or of California wine."

Swan still has its original tile floor and marble counter. Expect to stand in line for a seat.
(Christopher Cellars, 2011)

A. LA ROCCA SEA FOOD:
THE STORY OF THE CRAB KING

Accursio La Rocca on San Francisco Bay in a boat he ordered to be built in 1916.
(La Rocca family)

IN THE LATE NINETEENTH CENTURY, Accursio La Rocca came to San Francisco from Sciacca, Sicily, and before the quake, he began selling crabs out of a wheelbarrow to restaurants up the hill in North Beach and downtown. Within a few years, business was good enough that he could afford a horse and wagon. He taught himself English and adopted the nickname "Leo," and soon he was widely known as the "Crab King."

For a couple of weeks in December 1918, local newspapers were obsessed with the story of the Crab King, who was sued by Edward Edlin for $100,000 for "having alienated from him the affections of Mrs. Edlin." The stories fretted about the fact that women were on the jury and "were of an age and comeliness one does not normally associate with the sterner realities of justice," and reporters gave the helpful context that $100,000 was equal to the "profit on two million crabs."

Crab King Denies He Tampered With Mrs. Edlin's Affections

Women Jurors and Delicate English Feature Alienation Suit

The *San Francisco Chronicle* front page December 3, 1918, featured coverage of the trial.

The trial included sobbing – and even fainting – from Margaret Edlin as testimony about her relationships with other men dragged on for days. In the end, the jury found that the Crab King had indeed alienated Mrs. Edlin from her husband. But the judgment was determined to be only $1 – or about the cost of "three average crabs" – and not the $100,000 Mr. Edlin had sought. La Rocca's attorney offered to pay the fine on the spot.

Through the twentieth century, the A. La Rocca business continued to grow. Accursio's sons Alphonse and Pasquale helped explore ways to expand the area where they could deliver live crab. One family story goes that the brothers drove their dad's Stearns luxury sedan up north to Eureka in the late 1920s, took the back seats out, and came back with 100 pounds of live crab in the back to prove they could distribute that far away.

Eventually, the business grew from a wheelbarrow to 10 boats unloading up and down the coast, says Michael La Rocca, Accursio's great-grandson. Pasquale kept the company growing for decades – even teaching himself French so he could build relationships with more of the chefs in town.

Michael and his siblings started helping out their great-uncle while in their teens: "We would always come to the wharf, learning how to cut fish and how to buy fish," Michael remembers. Michael was only 20 and about to head to a Gonzaga University study-abroad program in Florence, Italy, in 1980 when Pasquale died. Instead of going to Italy, Michael returned to San Francisco to take over the business.

Alphonse La Rocca's children, Leo and Annette, about 1940. Leo is Michael La Rocca's father. (La Rocca family)

Michael, his brothers Nicholas and Paul, and their sister Laura still run A. La Rocca. These days, they buy seafood from around the world and distribute in a 100-mile radius around the Bay Area, and they have decades-long relationships with some of San Francisco's oldest restaurants. "It's not about selling the product," Michael says. "It's about getting it to them every day." He's often in the office by 2 a.m. so their fish can get to the restaurants in time for lunch.

The A. La Rocca offices are still on Fisherman's Wharf, where only a few families from the turn of the twentieth century are still in business. "We're the old ones now," Michael says.

A LEGACY BUILT ON BREAD

Owner Ambrogio Soracco, left, and a friend whose name has been lost over time stand in the bakery in its early years. (Soracco family)

"People love it because everything here is done by hand. We don't cut corners."

— Michael Soracco

Italian immigrants eat in a North Beach refugee camp after the 1906 earthquake.
(California Historical Society, FN-34262)

UP THE HILL IN NORTH BEACH, bread-heads flock to a tiny bakery that does one thing and does it extremely well: "You have to get the focaccia," says Brian Dwyer at Swan Oyster Depot as he shucks his way through a mountain of oysters. "And you have to eat it right there, warm, in the park." He grew up eating the Italian-style flatbread during breaks from school. "Get the pizza one."

Liguria Bakery has fed the neighborhood for more than a hundred years from its corner on Stockton Street across from Washington Square park. The original owner, Ambrogio Soracco, arrived from Genoa, Italy, about a year after the quake, when hundreds of refugees were still camped in Washington Square.

After the quake, some North Beach residents camped in Washington Square park, center. The corner directly behind the park's diagonal path is Filbert and Stockton, where Liguria Bakery would open in 1911. (San Francisco History Center, San Francisco Public Library)

Historians say the neighborhood rebuilt relatively quickly and continued to attract new arrivals during the rebuilding years. By 1910, the city had nearly 17,000 Italian immigrants, most of them from northern Italy and living in North Beach. It's unclear what exactly drew Ambrogio to San Francisco, but he quickly found work in other neighborhood bakeries and in 1911, he opened his own.

Ambrogio summoned two brothers from Genoa to join him in working the bakery. "They did pretty well," said Ambrogio's grandson, Michael Soracco, who runs the bakery today. Liguria sold to grocery stores in the neighborhood, "and they did a lot of home deliveries, first by horse and wagon." When Ambrogio died in 1938, the family's partners continued to run the operation until his son, George, started at the bakery full-time a few years later, right out of high school. George worked there for 66 years – walking into work many days until the last months before he died in 2013 at age 84. "That bakery was his life," Michael said.

Ambrogio Soracco, front left, his wife, Mary, standing behind his left shoulder, and extended family in the early twentieth century. (Soracco family)

During Liguria Bakery's first 50 years, the family baked Italian breads, breadsticks and rolls. The Soraccos always made focaccia, but originally it was more of an afterthought. Around 1960 they decided to focus exclusively on the focaccia. "It got hard for them to compete with the big bakeries," said Michael, who has worked full-time in the bakery since 1981. The bread continues to sell well, and in the past few years Michael has brought back the panettone as a special treat around Christmas. Customers snap it up quickly.

Now Michael fires up the original brick oven Tuesday through Saturday, turning out golden focaccia in flavors such as onion, raisin, jalapeño, rosemary — and yes, pizza, topped with tomato sauce and green onions. It's intensely physical work. He arrives around 3 a.m. weekdays – 1 a.m. Saturdays – to mix the dough in a white 100-year-old machine that resembles a small cement mixer. The recipe has been handed down, not written down, and for decades Michael was the only one who knew the mix.

Family friend Forrestt Vinson-Crivello helped the Soraccos with baking on busy
Saturdays for many years. Behind him is the original 101-year-old brick oven.
(Tandemvines Media, 2012)

The biggest batches take as much as 250 pounds of flour and make
roughly 500 pounds of dough. With this volume, the bakery buys its
fifty-pound sacks of flour 100 sacks at a time, continuing to purchase
from its original suppliers. "We stay loyal to the purveyors," Michael
said.

Once mixed, the massive blob of dough must be wrestled out and allowed to rise twice before it is divided into 20-by-30-inch pans, where
it rises a third time. Michael calculates how much of each type of focaccia to make based on which delis and restaurants they are delivering to
and what's selling in the front. He and a small handful of family members and friends who work with him rain tomato sauce, garlic, rosemary, and onions down onto the sheets of dough. The pizza topping is
the most popular, accounting for about half of what they sell.

Fourteen pans of focaccia at a time can fit into the brick oven, which
reaches to the ceiling.

Michael Soracco uses wooden paddles to move the sheets of fresh-baked focaccia from pan to cooling rack. His sister works behind him. (Tandemvines Media, 2012)

As bread bakes at 600 to 700 degrees in the oven and the ambient temperature in the back of the shop climbs above 90 degrees, Michael wields long wooden paddles to move the bread from the pans to the cooling racks, and then from the racks to a table, where it's sliced into roughly 8-by-10-inch sheets. Baking usually wraps up by 9 a.m. Once the bread is done, it's time to make deliveries to restaurants and delis.

In the front of the shop, Michael's sister, Mary Gephardt, and mother, Josephine Soracco, answer the phone and work the spare front counter, where they deftly wrap focaccia in plain white paper and tie it up with string.

Wrapped rectangles sit on the white shelves behind them stacked for takeout orders, looking like gifts. In between customers, Mary and Josephine catch up on Giants baseball news and neighborhood gossip. Most of the family except Michael still lives within a couple of blocks of the bakery.

The line of customers turns to a steady stream on Saturdays, and they are deeply loyal; one man in line had been buying bread at Liguria Bakery for 47 years. Liguria has never advertised – "Our product is our advertisement," Michael said – and has no website or email address.

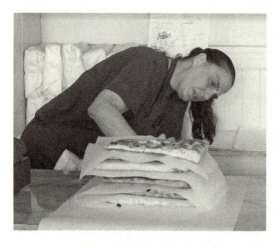

Between the walk-in line and call-in orders, Mary Gephardt, granddaughter of the original owner, must wrap quickly to keep up. (Tandemvines Media, 2012)

Despite the challenges of a changing neighborhood, competition from bigger bakeries, and low-carb diets, the word-of-mouth strategy still works and business is pretty decent. And when times have been leaner, "it helps that we're all family here," said Michael. The next generation of Soraccos has their hands in the mix, too: Michael's daughter, Leslie Mitchell, now works a couple of days a week at the bakery, and his nephew, Sonny Soracco, also helps out occasionally.

Michael said he can't afford to think about retiring – "I'm going to be here!" – but he has passed down the family recipe to his daughter.

As for San Franciscans' affection for the focaccia, Michael attributes that to the simple quality of the bread: "People love it because everything here is done by hand. We don't cut corners."

And does he still enjoy it after more than 35 years of making focaccia? "I wouldn't be doing it if I didn't."

Liguria Bakery closes early when it sells out. So go early, bring cash, and do as Brian says: Eat it warm, in the park.

1700 Stockton St.
415-421-3786
No website
Open Tuesday-Friday, 8 a.m. to 2 p.m. (or when the focaccia is gone), and Saturday, 7 a.m. to 1 p.m. The bakery closes between Christmas and New Year's, and often for a few weeks in the middle of the summer.

LIGURIAN FOCACCIA

(Christopher Cellars, 2011)

TODAY'S FOCACCIAS are descended from ancient "panis focacius" – meaning "hearth bread" in Latin – which was first baked on a stone slab in the hearth and covered in ashes. The olive oil-enriched, salted, soft flatbread we know now as focaccia is most closely identified with the Ligurian region of Italy – especially its capital city of Genoa, which Ambrogio Soracco left in 1907, destined for San Francisco's North Beach neighborhood.

In much of northern Italy, focaccia is better known as "pizza genovese" and is often topped with sauteed onions. Other regions of Italy have their own versions of focaccia. In Florence, Rome, and parts of central Italy, the flatbread is called "schiacciata," and it is "pinze" in the south. In Bologna, it's more likely to be known as "crescentina" and might come flecked with bacon. If you ask for "focaccia" there, you likely will receive a panettone-like cake instead.

At Liguria Bakery in San Francisco, the Soraccos make focaccia with ten different toppings: plain, onion, pizza, raisin, garlic, rosemary, mushroom, black olive, rosemary garlic and jalapeno cheese. Although the pizza topping is the best-seller at the shop by far, Michael says his family's favorite is the plain, which they enjoy as bread for sandwiches or on its own with dinner. "Plain is the best," he said. "You can taste the flavor of the bread."

– *Sources: "Essentials of Classic Italian Cooking," Marcella Hazan (A.A. Knopf, 2008); "The Italian Baker," Carol Field (Ten Speed Press, 2011).*

THE BOXERS' RENDEZVOUS

Jim Griffin referees the Ad Wolgast-Willie Ritchie lightweight title fight Nov. 28, 1912. Griffin called below-the-belt fouls on Wolgast in the 16th round, awarding the title to Ritchie. Griffin also owned the Andromeda Saloon – now the home of the Comstock Saloon on Columbus Avenue. (Bain News Service / Library of Congress)

"In our heads, it was 1910. We had a very romantic vision of what a pre-Prohibition bar was like: mustachioed bartenders dressed to the nines serving strong drinks. We were able to live that romance."

– Jonny Raglin, Comstock Saloon

The Comstock Saloon's Cuban mahogany bar top is believed to pre-date the 1906 quake.
(The Absinthe Group, 2017)

THE COMSTOCK SALOON WANTS TO BE Jim Griffin's kind of place. The décor is probably a bit more polished than the famed boxing referee's old haunts, but the drinks are true to pre-Prohibition form, the mustachioed bartenders look the part, and the jazz from the mezzanine keeps the bar loud and lively, just like in its Barbary Coast heyday.

Griffin first opened the Andromeda Saloon nearby on Kearney Street in the years before the quake. At the west edge of the red-light district named after the North Africa pirating region, the Andromeda was a "rendezvous of men of the fight game" among the saloons, gambling dens, dance halls and brothels that packed the three-block area.

Griffin was famous in the boxing world that dominated the sports news pages of the time. Although he had done some boxing in his youth,

"Firecracker Jim" really made his name as a fight promoter, referee and manager of the Broadway Athletic Club. After the 1906 earthquake and fires ravaged the neighborhood, Griffin rebounded quickly and in 1907 he opened the Andromeda at a new location up the street – in the building where the Comstock stands today.

Jim Griffin from his *Chronicle* obituary

The Red Light Abatement Act of 1914 tamed much of the Barbary Coast, but the Andromeda had a ringside seat in the boxing world into the 1920s. Tickets were sold there, boxers would weigh in before fights, and heavyweight champion Jack Dempsey was said to have worked there as a bouncer for a time around 1913.

The saloon became Andromeda Café during Prohibition, and legend has it that gangster George "Baby Face" Nelson, who spent some time in those years as a bootlegger north of the city, met with an Andromeda bartender.

When Griffin died in 1935, the *San Francisco Chronicle* gave tribute:

"Jim Griffin was said to have refereed more championship fights than any other man in America. From the days of John L. Sullivan and 'Gentleman' Jim Corbett he had known all and they all knew Jim Griffin. They gathered at his place down at 155 Columbus street and fought the fights ahead of time and fought and refought the current bouts and those of yesteryear – and Jim was an oracle of the ring."

Through the following decades, the saloon continued to draw patrons under many names. It was known as the La Planta in the early 1960s, and was a tropical-themed dive bar when Janis Joplin supposedly sang there one night. It became the Albatross in the 1970s and then the San Francisco Brewing Company in 1985.

(The Absinthe Group, 2017)

By the time Jonny Raglin heard the San Francisco Brewing Company was for sale in 2009, he and his partners at the Absinthe Group had been looking for a place to open a pre-Prohibition-style saloon for a few years. The building's solid construction and the distinctive bar top convinced them to buy it. "In the saloon, we had a no-nonsense, well-constructed place that frankly made sense in 2010."

Raglin's team kept several original fixtures. He believes the 18-foot Cuban mahogany bar top predates the 1906 quake, and says the Brunswick back bar could have been manufactured in the company's South San Francisco facility, which operated in the late nineteenth century. It's hard to know whether these pieces were in the first version of the Andromeda, but Raglin speculates the fixtures could have survived the fires if the owners had taken some protective measures when they realized the destruction that was headed their way. "They had time to save the bar," he said.

The renovation also preserved the urinal trough ringing the bottom of the bar – a now purely decorative nod to the saloon's men-only days, which lasted through Prohibition, Raglin said.

Some fixtures – like the punka wallah fans that turn lazily overhead – have been a part of the bar's atmosphere for decades, but Raglin isn't sure when they were added. For the lighting, molding and fixtures they needed to update, Raglin's team focused on the building's earliest years: "In our heads, it was 1910."

"We had a very romantic vision of what a pre-Prohibition bar was like: mustachioed bartenders dressed to the nines serving strong drinks. We were able to live that romance."

(Christopher Cellars, 2012)

The name was chosen in honor of the Comstock Lode – the 20-year silver strike discovered in Utah in 1859 that brought vast riches to San Francisco. "The story of the Comstock Lode hadn't been told," Raglin said.

To get a taste of the bar's pre-Prohibition roots, Raglin suggests three of the drinks on the Comstock's tightly edited cocktail menu:

THE MARTINEZ is a precursor to the martini that some say was first made in San Francisco and others say was created in Martinez, California. It incorporates Old Tom Gin, a style of gin that was popular in the late nineteenth century.

PISCO PUNCH, made from brandy brought to the city in Gold Rush years by ships stopping in Chile and Peru, is widely considered San Francisco's original signature cocktail. "It's also strangely good for the modern palate," Raglin said.

THE SAZERAC is often associated more closely with New Orleans, but Raglin said it was a ubiquitous, popular cocktail before Prohibition. "We're positive it was being served in San Francisco."

Comstock's take on the drinks has been adapted from the recipes of the time, Raglin said. "The palate is different now. People liked their drinks sweeter then." But the goal is to make the experience as authentic as possible.

And the live music every night is meant to honor the tradition of the Barbary Coast.

"We wanted to honor the bars that came before us."

155 Columbus Street
Phone: 415-617-0071
www.comstocksaloon.com

SAM WO, CHINATOWN

THE THREE HARMONIES

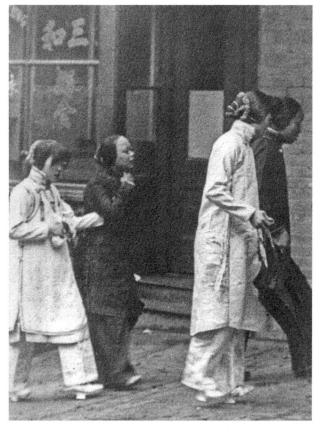

Women walk up Washington Street in front of the original Sam Wo in a photo dated between 1915 and 1935. The restaurant's name in Chinese characters can be seen on the top window. (Chinese Historical Society of America)

David Ho was the majority owner of Sam Wo in 2012, when he made rice-noodle rolls every day in the basement at 813 Washington St. (Tandemvines Media, 2012)

DOWN UNEVEN STEPS in a dim, damp basement, starting in the wee hours of the morning, David Ho made the specialty of the house. His narrow sliver of a restaurant, Sam Wo, had first opened in Chinatown a century ago – just a couple of years after the quake – and for decades it had been famous for Ho's handmade rice-noodle rolls. Every day, Ho soaked the rice, ground it to create "rice water," and ladled the white batter onto round metal trays, steaming them to create plate-sized noodles. He scattered barbecued pork, eggs, and cilantro on the noodles and swiftly rolled them with a graceful little flip to seal. On busy nights when the restaurant ran out of the noodle rolls, he would slip back downstairs after midnight and make a fresh batch.

David Ho and his daughter, Julie, look through family pictures the morning after the city informed them they would need to shut down. That day, the family thought they would be closing Sam Wo for good. (Tandemvines Media, 2012)

Ho made the customer favorites over and over in the basement on Washington Street for more than 30 years – until spring 2012, when he was forced to take a long break.

Any restaurant that manages to survive more than 100 years can expect some near-death experiences – moments when the owners must face the wear and tear of age on their buildings (and often themselves), take a deep breath, and decide if they can keep going. Sam Wo's owners faced such a moment on the 106th anniversary of the Great Quake.

On Wednesday, April 18, 2012, San Francisco health and fire inspectors told Ho and his daughter, Julie, who often translates for him, that the restaurant needed a mountain of work to bring it up to current codes. The family was stunned at the long list of violations.

They had been prepared to address standard restaurant issues raised about hygiene, food handling, and refrigeration. But larger structural deficiencies with the building and the equipment were a surprise and would require a daunting amount of money to address. The building's owner, Pui Yee Chan, was equally overwhelmed.

Ho bargained with the inspectors to get two more days to sell the restaurant's supplies of food, and then announced he would close the restaurant for good at the end of service that Friday night.

The day before the scheduled closure, Julie was heartbroken. "Everything we eat, sleep, and wear is from the restaurant," she said. "It's a death in the family." Her father was exhausted. "It's too old. Everything is too old," he said softly.

While Julie understood the safety concerns – "It would be the worst thing in the world if someone ever got sick" – that day as they faced closing their doors, she desperately wanted some special considerations from the city for Sam Wo's history. "It's been the way it has been for the last century. I don't know why they can't let it be."

Washington Street between Stockton and Grant (then called Dupont) after the quake. Within two years, Sam Wo would open on this block. The ruins of the Hall of Justice building are at center. (California Historical Society, FN-34907)

SAM WO'S ROOTS go back to the rush to rebuild Chinatown in the years right after the 1906 earthquake. While the neighboring North Beach area recovered quickly, it was only because of the community's resolve that Chinatown recovered at all. That spring, it was "a heap of smoking ruins," reported the Oakland Tribune. Looting was rampant and no one knew exactly how many people had died there.

As the rest of the city started to rebuild, newspaper editorial pages nationwide, from *The New York Times* to the *Cleveland Plain Dealer,* pushed a movement to relocate San Francisco's Chinatown to the mud flats of Hunter's Point, miles from downtown. But Chinese politicians and businessmen threatened to take their business to another West Coast city like Seattle or Los Angeles, and won the fight to rebuild downtown.

Once the neighborhood's location was secured, the family, district, and fraternal associations that ran Chinatown quickly mustered the manpower and resources to rebuild. One of the most prominent merchants, Look Tin Eli, raised millions of dollars in Hong Kong for the recovery.

Within a couple of years, the streets bustled again, this time with brightly lit, exotic buildings designed to attract white tourists – introducing the pagoda-themed look the neighborhood still has.

It was during this period that tiny Sam Wo started serving customers in its narrow building on Washington Street. "It's always been Sam Wo, and it's always served rice porridge [jook], which is a Chinese breakfast food," Julie Ho said.

Sam Wo's food was hearty and cheap: jook with broth of duck or beef, beef organs, rice noodles. In the 1940s and '50s, the restaurant gave away leftovers after closing time, Julie said. "Because it was so affordable, it's the place people would go to when they had practically nothing in their pockets."

From the beginning, Sam Wo had multiple owners who held shares in the restaurant. The name – pronounced "sam whoa" – means "three harmonies" in Chinese. One story goes that the name came from three siblings from Taishan in southern China who first opened it. Julie also likes another version of the story – that the restaurant operates with three harmonies to be successful: Heaven (interpreted as weather), Earth (location), and Man (customers).

The third harmony came through in a big way for Sam Wo in 2012.

WHEN WORD SPREAD that the restaurant would be closing, customers from throughout the Bay Area rushed to Chinatown. Hundreds stood in line for hours those two nights in April to enjoy one last dinner, a bowl of *jook* or rice noodle rolls. While waiting, they shared their stories and memories: "My grandparents ate here." "My parents loved Sam Wo.

I have to tell my dad!" "I can't believe it. I've been coming here since the '60s." And over and over: "I had to come one more time."

Some longtime customers who started coming in the 1950s when Sam Wo was hip among the Beat Generation knew about a secret menu: If they asked, they might get duck noodle rolls or shrimp noodle rolls instead of the barbecued pork noodle rolls listed on the menu.

Edsel Ford Fung, the famous "world's rudest waiter," in 1980 with Sydney, a customer who sent the restaurant this photo. (Ho family)

Others remembered Edsel Ford Fung, a waiter from the 1960s to the '80s who was once christened the "world's rudest waiter" by *San Francisco Chronicle* columnist Herb Caen. Fung was famous for harassing customers, especially women, and made a cameo in Armistead Maupin's serialized *Tales of The City*. "Edsel was just part of the show," Julie said. Long after Fung's death in 1984, giving customers a hard time stayed part of the restaurant's culture, and those waiting in line those last nights shared stories of playful abuse. Julie, who also had a job as a rehab nurse, loved dishing it out. "Here I got to be the waitress that yells at people," she said. "It's kept me balanced."

On Friday, April 20, 2012, customers waited for hours in a line that stretched around the block. Sam Wo sold all of its food before closing at 3 a.m. (Tandemvines Media, 2012)

On the closing Friday night, customers crammed the upstairs tables and the line stretched around the block and down Grant Avenue. By 3 a.m. Saturday, the restaurant managed to squeeze in everyone who was waiting, and they sold all the food. At the end, the servers were cobbling together plates from random items from the kitchen, Julie said. "Half the people didn't mind."

The outpouring was a break the Ho family needed. Without the lines of people showing their support, the health inspector probably wouldn't have reached out to them on the Friday they closed, offering an opportunity to discuss the restaurant's issues in a public hearing.

"We're lucky to have the history we have," Julie said. "We wouldn't have had the chance if we were any other business."

More importantly, it gave her dad the energy to fight for the restaurant. Worn out from so many long hours over more than three decades, David Ho was almost ready to give up on Sam Wo. But after he saw the lines outside, the crowd at the public hearing the next week, and the offers of help from the community, Julie said, "I've seen some fire in my dad that I hadn't seen before."

"My dad says, 'Now the restaurant is not just the Ho family. It's the community. It's San Francisco.'"

OFFERS OF HELP STREAMED IN from longtime customers, city politicians, and agencies like the Chinatown Community Development Center. Entertainment Commissioner Steven Lee, a businessman known for revitalizing the old Trocadero Transfer nightclub, came to David Ho right away and said, "Whatever help you need, you can get it from me."

Through those first months, the family struggled to navigate the bureaucracy and the vastly different opinions about how to approach the work that needed to be done. As meetings were delayed and the summer dragged on, they also struggled with the waiting. "My dad isn't used to not doing stuff," Julie said midsummer. "And we're all gaining weight!"

Sam Wo wasn't a typical project for the nonprofit CCDC, but the executive director, Rev. Norman Fong, took up the restaurant's cause because it was a special place to him. Growing up in Chinatown, he had eaten at Sam Wo all his life. And during the 1970s, when he had his own band, he and his bandmates spent many late nights at the restaurant. "I'm just in this because I love the place."

And he was troubled by other recent closures of longtime businesses. Rev. Fong believed Sam Wo's fate was important to the neighborhood. "It's the history of Chinatown. We can't let everything go."

For several months after the closing, he coordinated efforts for the Ho family, working behind the scenes with the city and offering project-management help. He also worked with organizations like the nonprofit Asian Neighborhood Design and businesses that had expertise in customizing equipment for Chinatown's old buildings. He admitted having moments when he was unsure whether Sam Wo could be saved, but "if it doesn't work, at least we gave 1,000 percent effort."

And while the overwhelming response of the community reflected the love for the restaurant, a few Chinatown residents said quietly that places like Sam Wo were painful reminders of a time when racial discrimination kept options for the city's Chinese population limited to small restaurants and laundries. But Rev. Fong countered: "This is a respect for the past. It was tough and depressing sometimes, but so what? That's part of our past."

That fall, Sam Wo had a breakthrough: Its plan for building improvements received the green light from the city departments that had raised the issues in April. But early estimates placed the costs at $100,000 – much more than the Ho family had. They explored loans, but still needed to raise tens of thousands of dollars. They planned their first fundraiser – a luncheon featuring dishes from the restaurant. "We need to have the community to rebuild Sam Wo," Rev. Fong said.

The hope was that the restaurant would be able to open within a few months.

BUT BY THE END OF THE YEAR, it was clear that it would take far more than $100,000 to upgrade the building. With an architect and contractor lined up, the new estimate was $300,000. The Ho family and their advocates proposed that the building owner pay $100,000 and Sam Wo would pay the rest. The building owner had never had to contribute to the building maintenance before, and she wasn't interested in starting. The owner also insisted on a huge rent increase, and negotiations stalled.

As the months stretched into 2013 and the first anniversary of the closure passed, businessman Steven Lee started taking a larger role in helping the Ho family weigh their options. They considered partnering with a bar. Maybe a food truck. Several times the family considered giving up. "Dad expressed that it might be best for him to sell the restaurant," Julie said that spring. "He said he doesn't mind selling, thinking of all of us."

Lee and others in the community urged them to keep going. Lee began proposing a new group of partners for the restaurant ownership to bring in an infusion of cash and save Sam Wo. The investors would get the rights to the Sam Wo name and recipes with an eye to eventually creating a frozen-food line; the Ho family would provide their expertise and keep a piece of the ownership.

Julie Ho's great-grandfather, Hay Go, bought into the restaurant in the late 1960s.
(Ho family)

The family worried that the investors would change the restaurant's character. One of the investors wanted to attract a younger crowd and more tourists – and to raise the prices. "The main concern for me is that we keep the integrity of the restaurant," Julie said. "We want it to be meaningful. Sam Wo is history, not just a brand."

But by summer, the family was working with Lee and his partner Jonathan Leong on finalizing the investment plan. Sam Wo Ventures was formed and the Sam Wo name was trademarked. "Our family wants Sam Wo, the history, to continue on. Steven Lee can help us," Julie said.

THE HO FAMILY got into the group ownership of Sam Wo in the late 1960s when Julie's great-grandfather, Hay Go, bought a share from a member of Edsel Ford Fung's family – a man whom Go had befriended in

Chinatown's gambling parlors. David Ho emigrated from China in 1981 and started work in the restaurant so he could help his siblings and parents move to America. Ho took over his family's share in the late 1980s and became the majority owner and manager.

Julie started in the restaurant when she was only 9, when her dad set her to chopping vegetables and answering phones because she complained that she was bored. "I grew up there," she said. Her brother, mom, and other family members also have worked there.

In summer 2013, as the Sam Wo ownership was changing again – and plans for reopening languished – Julie was pregnant with her first child. "My life has been in the restaurant. I would love to have this baby grow up there."

But it wouldn't be on just one family to save Sam Wo, Julie said. "It has to be a group effort."

Julie Ho's grandfather, Ying Xiang He, in front of the restaurant in the early 1990s.
(Ho family)

IN AUGUST 2013, the owner of 813 Washington Street put the old building up for sale. "It was a relief even though it was a surprise," Julie said. "The landlady wasn't understanding what the restaurant is about."

Some of the investors dropped out when they learned Sam Wo couldn't return to its historic home. Lee and the Ho family had already considered that they might need to find a new location – but they agreed that it had to be in Chinatown.

"We can't move outside Chinatown," Lee said. He wanted to keep Sam Wo alive for the Ho family – but he also wanted to bring something back to the neighborhood that he felt had been lost.

Lee was a student at San Francisco State University in the late 1970s the first time he ate at Sam Wo. He had grown up in the small town of Vacaville, California, and he fell in love with Chinatown nightlife. "Walking down the street then, Chinatown was a really busy place." While still in college, Lee was already putting on events and working as a DJ, and Sam Wo was a popular spot to get a cheap bite to eat late at night after shows.

Over the years as he became a partner in nightclubs, Lee had been a regular customer at Sam Wo – and had watched the nightlife of Chinatown steadily fade away. "Chinatown was slowly dying," he said. "A lot of the old restaurants were owned by old families. You had a business in Chinatown so your kids can get out of Chinatown."

Lee saw the community's passion for Sam Wo when it closed, and also saw a business opportunity. He was determined to help the Ho family reopen the restaurant and breathe some nightlife back into the neighborhood.

So, Lee and the Ho family looked for the right place in Chinatown. They had to be patient.

IT WAS THE END OF 2014 – more than two and a half years after Sam Wo closed – when a suitable location presented itself. The owner of Anna's Bakery on Clay Street was looking to retire. The bakery was in a newer building than the original Sam Wo, of course, but the space felt right. It had a narrow main floor and an upstairs for dining. Not too fancy. A kitchen in the basement was twice as wide – gargantuan by Sam Wo standards.

The building was closer to the Financial District, and Lee saw potential in the lunch crowd traffic. It was owned by one of Chinatown's family associations, which offered a reasonable lease.

Most of the restaurant's previous staff had moved on to other jobs, but David Ho planned to train a new staff of cooks in Sam Wo's traditional recipes and techniques. "I'm happy there's an outlet for him to pass it on without us having to keep it alive on our own," Julie said.

Julie worried about balancing the needs of her 1-year-old son with her nursing job and the demands of reopening the restaurant. "I'm super nervous about how it will all play out," she said.

The biggest relief was that Anna's Bakery was an operational restaurant. The Sam Wo group estimated it would take only about three months to convert the restaurant to serve the rice-noodle rolls, *jook* and other favorites. Plans were made to buy the bakery.

THE MONEY WAS STILL IN ESCROW in March 2015 when the Sam Wo ownership learned that Anna's Bakery had been operating illegally. The city Health Department had ordered the restaurant closed the previous fall, but the owner had ignored the inspectors and didn't tell the Ho family that her business wasn't in compliance. "It's a gutsy, ballsy thing to sell a business that isn't real," Julie fumed.

The kitchen needed substantial work to pass health inspections. It had home-grade rather than restaurant-grade freezers. The prep tables had wood where there should be stainless steel. A pizza oven the size of a small dinosaur would need to be removed. And there were rats.

The Sam Wo owners renegotiated the deal with the owner of Anna's Bakery. In the end, they would pay her a quarter of the original price for the business. The remaining money would go toward the needed upgrades.

When Julie despaired about the extra work, Lee offered encouragement: "Julie, in the past couple of years, you've learned some things that some people will never learn in a lifetime."

David and Julie Ho were exhausted the night before Sam Wo reopened in the old Anna's Bakery space on Clay Street. (Tandemvines Media, 2015)

LEE HAD AN AMBITIOUS PLAN to reopen in the new space July 1. But the old oven had to have a new hood. The Robert Yick Company, known for making Chinese restaurant equipment in San Francisco since 1910, would make a new steamer for the rice-noodle rolls. A point-of-sale computer system for orders had to be installed. A whole new staff had to be hired and trained.

David and Julie Ho started to realize that they weren't reopening the old restaurant so much as starting up a new restaurant. "Before, everything was a more traditional Chinese business," Julie said. "Now everything has to be an open book."

But there were some historic touches from the old place they all insisted on. A dumbwaiter had to be installed to move dishes between floors. And Sam Wo had to fight to get its historic neon sign back from the original building.

The shiny new kitchen slowly came together over the summer. Lee made new wood tops for the dining tables and signed the back side – "In case a hundred years from now, the tables are still there," Julie said.

Julie relied heavily on friends, like Jane Fong, who pitched in at all hours to get the restaurant ready. "We're very lucky to have this many people come forward to support us," Julie said over and over.

Late in the summer, as Sam Wo's ownership wrestled over prices – the new investors pushed for higher prices and the family fought to keep them low, per Sam Wo tradition – an astrologer chose an auspicious date for the official opening.

But maybe even more momentous would be the date of the last health inspection to pass before opening. "When the health inspector finally was giving approval to the new location, she said to my dad, 'This is the kitchen you deserve.' " Julie paused. "That was a really nice thing to translate for my dad."

ALMOST EXACTLY THREE AND A HALF YEARS after Sam Wo closed – on the astrologer-approved date of October 21, 2015 – the restaurant reopened on Clay Street across from Portsmouth Square Plaza, two blocks from its historic home. Politicians and community leaders made speeches. Lion dancers wound through the crowd packed onto the sidewalk and into the restaurant, and confetti rained down. Julie's 2-year-old son, Ethan, cut the ribbon.

And the old customers came. Ron Faulkner, sitting on a stool on the sidewalk watching the festivities, had talked his way into a box of the first rice-noodle rolls of the day, hours before Sam Wo officially opened. Daniel Soo Hoo, a retired postal service worker, said he'd been coming to Sam Wo since junior high days. "Sam Wo isn't important just to Chinatown," he said as he enjoyed lunch from the celebration buffet. "It's important to San Francisco as a whole."

As they ate, many there on opening day lingered over the photographs on the walls. There were the images showing Sam Wo's long history and favorite characters like Edsel Ford Fung – and there were photos celebrating how the community had rallied when Sam Wo shut down in 2012.

Julie and her dad were exhausted. They had to work through a lot of snags in the last days before the opening. At one point right before the opening, the noodle steamer broke down. They were desperately short of staff – and the staff they had still didn't know the new ordering systems or how exactly to make the food to David Ho's standards. But they all savored the moment. "We want this to last," Julie said. "It's the end of one struggle. It's a beginning, too."

Steven Lee smiles in the middle of the crowd of politicians, customers and media as Sam Wo officially opens October 21, 2015. (Tandemvines Media, 2015)

IT TOOK SOME TIME for the new Sam Wo to find its rhythm. Old customers complained at first that the food didn't taste the same as it did at the old place and that the prices were too high, and the investors complained that Yelp reviews weren't as positive as they'd like. "Customers have a romantic way of seeing our food, and it doesn't taste the same," Julie said. When they complained, she would taste the food to learn what was wrong, so she could better describe an issue to the kitchen.

David Ho worked up to 20 hours a day cooking and trying to get the kitchen staff trained. He was especially frustrated with the cooks at first. Most of them had learned to stir-fry at a hotter temperature than he wanted, and they resisted learning his style. Sam Wo's taste comes from more of a slow-cook stir-fry. The food needs to braise a bit to develop the right flavors, he said.

A few months after the reopening, Julie and David Ho take a break upstairs to enjoy a late lunch of jook with Julie's son, Ethan. (Tandemvines Media, 2016)

Ho had learned how to cook by watching the other cooks at the old Sam Wo when he arrived as a young man in the early 1980s. "Back then, people didn't want to teach," Julie said. "Now, he's willing to teach and people are not willing to learn."

In an effort to balance work and family, Julie made the hard decision to limit her nursing job to a few days a month, and she was grateful that the hospital allowed her the flexibility: "Even though there are a lot of tears and frustration, I feel like this is more important than nursing right now. I want to be there for the restaurant," she said. "If it doesn't work out, at least I tried."

To make things easier, she eventually enrolled Ethan in a preschool a few blocks from the restaurant.

A few months into the new location, Sam Wo started to settle into a groove. The old customers were there, giving pointers – helpful and not. "We have a lot of old-timers coming back," Julie said. "They find it weird the place is so clean."

And new customers started coming up from the Financial District. The lunch hour – historically not Sam Wo's busiest time – started drawing crowds.

At the CCDC new year luncheon in February, 2016, the Ho family, the Sam Wo investors and the landlords were all honored for restoring the restaurant to Chinatown. (Tandemvines Media, 2016)

The kitchen staff grew more confident, and more of the old items returned to the menu. The raw-fish salad, a traditional dish for Chinese New Year, came back in time for the first new year in the new space.

That February, the community celebrated Sam Wo's revival: At the CCDC's new year luncheon, the group honored the family, the investors and Nam Ping Benevolent Association, the landlords of the building, for bringing the restaurant back to the community. As hundreds applauded, Lee told the crowd, "It's not so much sometimes the money; it's what's in our hearts."

More old traditions slowly returned. In April, the historic neon sign was finally restored and installed in the new location. The late hours for Friday and Saturday nights came back that first summer with a new touch: security to protect staff and patrons.

And new traditions were started. Customers could buy Sam Wo hot mustard and merchandise like t-shirts. By the end of 2016, the restaurant was selling beer and wine – something the old Sam Wo had never done. In 2017, David Ho started making the restaurant's own barbecued pork. And a photo booth was added so visitors could record their own memories.

TODAY, SAM WO ENJOYS a steady business and regularly appears on "best" lists like Eater SF's Essential 38 Restaurants and cheap eats lists. It has a solid 4-star rating on Yelp, and there is talk of eventually adding a second location in a domestic terminal at San Francisco International Airport. The investors still hope to get Sam Wo foods into grocery stores and are looking for a partner.

At the restaurant, Julie worries that her dad is still working long hours, and says they're talking him into at least relinquishing some of the cleaning duties. "My dad still has a lot to learn about delegating."

But even as he holds on to so much of the work, he reminds his daughter and business partners that he hopes to retire. Sometime soon. "To find the right new Mr. Ho has become the task," Lee says.

The Clay Street renovations are all paid for, and shareholders are pleased with their investment, Lee says: "The investors are happy for the community. They're happy to give a business back to a family. And happy to be bringing nightlife back to Chinatown."

As for Julie, she hopes to be able to devote more time to her nursing career at some point: "I love it a lot, and I don't want to give that up. But I'm not ready to give up the restaurant." And it's important to preserve time for Ethan, who now is quite vocal about his favorite Sam Wo foods. (Barbecued pork and dry mix noodles. And no vegetables!)

Julie still relies heavily on her friend, Jane Fong, who helps tag-team the management duties, but she knows she needs to hire someone so Fong can refocus on her graphic-design career. "It's hard to find an employee who would care as much as someone who's involved with the family," Julie says.

And as happy as she is to see the restaurant thriving, Julie worries a little that in the bustle, the Sam Wo story is getting lost. "Sometimes it gets so busy, I don't have time to educate the staff about what Sam Wo is about," she says. She wants them to be able to engage with the old customers who still come in and order their favorites.

"Everyone is really busting their butts and there's not much storytelling going on. But then again, if there's too much storytelling going on, things don't get done."

David Ho in his new Sam Wo kitchen. (Christopher Cellars, 2017)

As the century-old restaurant prepared to celebrate its second anniversary in its new space, David Ho took time in a television interview to look back on Sam Wo's long history. He had tears in his eyes as he recalled in Cantonese how the restaurant was saved: "So many people helped and supported us." And he gave his take on the three harmonies – the three elements that have made Sam Wo successful: the right place, the right time and the right people.

"I hope this story can keep going," he said. "Sam Wo remains its traditional style. I hope it can keep pace with the changing society."

713 Clay St., between Grant and Kearney
415-989-8898
www.samworestaurant.com

THE STORY OF THE RAW FISH SALAD

Julie Ho says Sam Wo's raw fish salad is a unique dish with a history that goes back to the early decades of the twentieth century. Here's the story behind the specialty, told by Julie with her dad, David Ho:

"ALTHOUGH WE SERVE IT YEAR ROUND, our raw fish salad is a special, traditional dish that we serve on a grander scale on the seventh day of Chinese New Year. The seventh day is known as *yun yut,* translating to People's Day, which means in the lunar calendar the birthday of the human race. Since this day is our 'birthday,' we should celebrate it by eating and doing things that encourage a good year. Eating the raw fish salad would be one of these things, especially if you were a gambler in the early 1900s in Chinatown.

Yu Saung is Cantonese for raw fish salad. *Yu* means fish; *Saung* means raw, but sounds like the word "alive." *Yu* in Cantonese sounds like a character meaning "wish" in a good-luck kind of way.

San Francisco's Chinatown of the early 1900s had a lot of underground gambling dens. Any kind of underground business is known in Cantonese as *lowe ga.* The Chinese character "lowe" sounds like the action of mixing. When you put that all together: People of the underground gambling industry (which was likely a good portion of the Chinese in Chinatown at the time) would get together on their "birthdays" (the seventh day of New Year) to have the raw fish salad in order to bring good luck for the new year. Part of the superstition is that one must mix (*lowe*) your own salad to get your wish.

Decades ago, the raw fish salad used to be made with steelhead, and old-timers still talk about how good that was. Today, it's made with tilapia.

Our everyday raw fish salad dish has the seasoned raw fish slices laid out and topped with piles of sweetly pickled cucumbers and melon, sesame seeds, crushed peanuts, pickled strips of yellow ginger, and, everyone's favorite, crunchy vermicelli noodles. Chopped cilantro and red-dyed chopped ginger as garnish.

The special raw fish salad for Chinese New Year has the ingredients mentioned above with these added: shreds of raw carrots, shreds of raw white radish, small pickled bulbs of onions (about olive-sized, with an explosion of sweet, sour, and spiciness), and, last but not least, strips of fried won ton wraps. There would be different prices of the "special" raw fish salad.

In the past decades that I've helped at the restaurant, on the seventh day of Chinese New Year, the associations from around Chinatown would order the special raw fish salad alongside a huge pot of porridge and Chinese doughnuts. Families that had the tradition of eating the fish salad would take a special trip to the restaurant to eat it. In recent New Year's celebrations, there haven't been as many requests for these traditional gatherings with the fish salad and porridge. Nonetheless, we still got old-timers and newbies enjoying the raw fish salad any time of the year, including myself."

THE PALACE HOTEL, MARKET STREET

GRANDEST IN THE WEST

More than 700 of San Francisco's most prominent men attended the reopening banquet
on Dec. 15, 1909. (Palace Hotel)

*"There, sitting at the banquet board, the remnants of the last years of care,
of struggle and strife against adversity were swept away. San Francisco,
which had fallen, had risen again. The Palace hotel, dearest spot in the city,
was once again."*

– The San Francisco Call, December 16, 1909

In 1887, the Palace had already been open for 12 years and was considered the premier hotel of the West. (Palace Hotel)

"**WE COULD SCARCELY THINK** of San Francisco without thinking of the Palace Hotel."

The mayor spoke these words in 1909 at the hotel's grand reopening three years after it was destroyed in the fires sweeping the city after the quake. But they could have been spoken at any point in the Palace's two lifetimes.

Before and after 1906, the Palace Hotel has been an emotional touchstone for the city. In its earliest days, locals took visitors to the "world's grandest hotel" to show off their city's success. When the Palace burned in 1906, newspapers screamed the news. And more than a century later, when the hotel's ownership planned to sell the beloved Maxfield Parrish mural hanging above its bar, citizens launched a passionate protest, calling the bar and its painting "the essence of San Francisco."

In 1875, when the Palace Hotel first rose on the corner of Market and New Montgomery, San Francisco was in the midst of one of its many construction booms. About 2,000 new buildings went up along with the hotel that year, and the Palace was the giant of the group. It had room for more than a thousand guests, making it the largest hotel in the West. The seven-story design was said to have been inspired by hotels in Vienna – though the bay windows looking out from every room were a distinctly San Franciscan touch – and it boasted an enormous courtyard with a driveway that deposited guests inside the building. Soon it was a destination for the rich and famous, drawing powerful businessmen and celebrities from Oscar Wilde to Rudyard Kipling:

> "The early pages of the Palace register contained the signatures
> of dozens of currently eminent figures in the nation's upbuilding:
> bankers, railroad-owners, steamship and mining magnates,
> lumbermen, promoters of every hue. A free-spending, hard-drinking
> group, 'self-made' almost to a man, they used the hotel's best suites as
> a base of operations."
> –Bonanza Inn: America's First Luxury Hotel

The hotel aspired to culinary excellence, hiring as its first chef Jules Harder, bringing a decade of experience at the famed Delmonico's restaurant in New York. But the Palace's biggest early epicurean influence came from exposing travelers to uniquely Californian dishes. Its menus routinely featured regional specialties like quail, venison and even grizzly steaks – along with the petite California oyster and abalone. In 1899, chef Fred Mergenthaler told a *San Francisco Examiner* reporter, "California oysters are beginning to be very much liked. California oyster cocktails are now famous all over the world."

IN SPRING 1906, the hotel was such a success that there was talk of adding two more floors, increasing the number of rooms to 1,200.

Because it was built just a few years after the 1868 quake, the building had been designed with earthquakes in mind, incorporating iron rods to reinforce its thick brick walls. So, when the quake struck early on April 18, the sturdy building appeared to have more cosmetic damage than deep structural weaknesses.

Dozens of survivor accounts set the scene that day. Opera tenor Enrico Caruso stayed at the Palace after performing in *Carmen* the previous night, and later described the early-morning terror to a London paper: "As the rocking continues, I get up and go to the window, raise the shade and look out. And what I see makes me tremble with fear. I see the buildings toppling over, big pieces of masonry falling, and from the street below I hear the cries and screams of men and women and children."

Alfred Hertz, *Carmen's* conductor, told of rushing outside to Market Street:

> *"The street presented an amazing series of grotesque sights. The majority of people had fled from their rooms without stopping to dress, many of them a little less than naked. But excitement was running so high that nobody noticed or cared.*
>
> *"The weather was beautiful but extremely cold. After standing for perhaps half an hour on Market Street, I felt so chilly that I took the suggestion of our first cellist, that we get something to warm us up at a nearby saloon. Before we realized what we had done, we found that we had consumed a whole quart of whiskey, and while under ordinary circumstances such an amount of alcohol might have killed me, this actually gave me sufficient courage to climb back to my room and get some clothes."*
>
> *—Bonanza Inn: America's First Luxury Hotel*

In the first hours after the quake, it appeared that the hotel would be out of service for only a few days. But as fires south of Market merged and began to devour the business district, the hotel staff realized that the building's dedicated 675,000-gallon reservoir wouldn't be enough to save it. By late afternoon, the Palace was overtaken by the flames. "PALACE HOTEL ON FIRE," the *Oakland Tribune* cried in its evening edition on Wednesday, April 18.

The Palace Hotel burns after the earthquake. (Pillsbury Picture Co., Library of Congress)

The ruins of the hotel after the April 18 earthquake and fires. (Palace Hotel)

An unnamed survivor watched the city burn: "Most impressive was the sight when the Palace Hotel went up in flames. This famous hostelry had been built in a manner intended to defy all the elements. ... What was remarkable in this spectacle was the varitety [sic] of colors in the flames."

The burning hotel and the charred shell left afterward were among the most-photographed ruins in the city, and hundreds of images survive.

The Palace Hotel reopened in 1909. (Palace Hotel)

OWNER FREDERICK SHARON, son of original owner William Sharon, quickly vowed to rebuild, choosing to tear down the surviving structure rather than build within it. The demolition alone cost $100,000. Sharon hired New York architect George Kelham of Trowbridge and Livingston as the project supervisor. Over the next couple of decades, Kelham would make over much of San Francisco, designing several more buildings and taking on the role of lead architect for the master plan of the 1915 Panama-Pacific International Exposition.

Kelham's Palace Hotel project was completed in about three and a half years, and today's magnificent Garden Court restaurant — the marble columns, the soaring glass Beaux Arts ceiling — is the same space celebrated in days of newspaper coverage in December 1909.

A 1915 banquet to honor Thomas Edison included telegraph keys to place orders.
(Palace Hotel)

At the time of the new Palace's first banquet, *The Call* wrote, "The spirit queen of San Francisco came to her absolute rule last night when the doors of the rebuilt Palace hotel swung open and more than 700 of her chieftains, leaders in her every walk of life, assembled within the domed court to pay homage and to acclaim the enthroning with banquet, song and laughter."

Attendees paid $15 apiece for the feast, and Mayor Edward Robeson Taylor spoke: "Lovers of San Francisco — The Palace Hotel has risen again, and we are here tonight to celebrate its Easter. ... The beauty of its architecture together with the spirit of hospitality which made the old hotel so justly famous, makes this new Palace Hotel as much an institution of San Francisco as is its City Hall, so that we could scarcely think of San Francisco without thinking of the Palace Hotel."

At the time, the grand dining space was called the Palm Court, and the restaurant hired only male staff and often held events open only to men. In 1915, a banquet hosted by California telephone operators honoring Thomas Edison included menus written in Morse code and orders placed with telegraph keys along wires strung from table to table. American presidents from Woodrow Wilson to John F. Kennedy have feasted at the hotel, and the banquet celebrating the opening session of the United Nations in 1945 was held here.

The Garden Court is San Francisco Landmark No. 18. The ceiling holds more than
70,000 pieces of colored glass; the chandeliers are Austrian crystal.
(Christopher Cellars, 2017)

Today, the Garden Court is open to anyone who wants to splurge for
lunch or linger over an afternoon coffee in its lounge area.

The full room stretches over more than 8,000 square feet, with the ceiling revealing the sky through more than 7,000 pieces of colored glass. The
columns and floor are Italian marble, and the chandeliers – some six feet
tall – are Austrian crystal. A 1991 renovation included structural repairs
after the 1989 Loma Prieta quake, but the Palace restored original features
and kept décor reflecting the sensibility of the early twentieth century.

The Garden Court is still the only indoor historic landmark in San
Francisco. "You're looking at what they saw when the hotel reopened,"
hotel spokeswoman Renée Roberts said.

The Sharon family owned the hotel until 1954, when the property was
sold to Sheraton, whose winning bid of $6.5 million bested Conrad Hil-
ton by $2 million. Currently owned by the Kyo-ya Corporation, the hotel
was updated in 2015, with furnishings refreshed throughout it. The hotel
regularly offers historic tours, and visitors should keep an eye out for the
resident ghost – a woman in a turn-of-the-century red dress who is said to
linger in the halls behind the French Parlor area, above the Garden Court.

Cover Charge 10 cents per person including Dry Toast, Rolls or Muffins
Toasted Rolls, Raisin Bread or Melba Toast—Buttered 15 cents
Imported French Gluten Bread 15 cents

MONDAY, OCTOBER 26, 1925

SPECIALTIES FOR TO-DAY

RELISHES

Tomato Jelly, Asparagus Tips 45	Hors d'Oeuvres, Palace 75	Ripe Olives 25
Jumbo Ripe Olives 35	Young's Superior Utah Celery 50	Fillet of Sand Dab in Aspic 75

Captain Cook Mackerel 60

OYSTERS

Milk Stew 70   Fried 75   Pan Roast 70

SOUPS

Consomme Noodles 30   Lentils Frankfort 30
Clam Broth 40   Mock Turtle 35   Chicken Broth 40   Chicken Okra 45   Petite Marmite 45

FISH

Sand Dab Meuniere 60   Baked Fillet of Sole Maude Adams 70   Halibut Hollandaise 70
Broiled Fresh Mackerel, Bacon 65   Boned Smelts, Tartar Sauce 60
Fried Scallops 85 Meuniere or Poulette 1.25   Cold Salmon, Mayonnaise 65
Lobster Cold or Broiled 1.35 Thermidor or Palace 1.50

ENTREES

Scrambled Egg, Creamed Ham 60   Roast Rack of Lamb Bouquetiere 95
Corned Beef Hash Browned, Fried Egg 60   Baked Oysters Waldorf 85
Chicken Croquette, Cream Sauce, New String Beans 60
Lamb Tongue with Fresh Mushrooms Poulette, Risotto 65
Hungarian Beef Goulash, Spatzen 55   Vegetable Dinner 50

ROASTS

Roast Turkey 1.30   Lamb, Mint Sauce 80   Ribs of Lamb 90   Ribs of Beef 90

SALADS

Palace Grill 65; Half 35   Green Goddess 50; Half 35   Lettuce 45; Half 25   Riverside 65; Half 35
Field 45 ½ 25 Chicken 1.00 Escarole 45; Half 25 Chicory 45; Half 25 Heart of Palms 90; ½ 50
Celery Root 45 ½ 25   Lobster 1.30 ½ 75 Louie 1.40 ½ 80   Celery, Palace 50; ½ 30

VEGETABLES

Creamed Spinach 40	English 40	Wild Rice 50	Polonaise 60	Boiled Onions 40
Cepes Saute 75	Stewed Corn 40	Egg Plant 40		Macaroni au Gratin 40
Imported Flageolets or String Beans 50		Cauliflower, Hollandaise 50		Fried Zucchini 40
New Peas or String Beans 60		Brussels Sprouts 45		Hubbard Squash 50

DESSERTS

Pumpkin, Cocoanut Custard or Apple Pie 25   Deep Cherry Pie 30   Strawberry Shortcake 50
Peach and Farina Pudding 30   Apple Cake with Whipped Cream 30   Marshmallow Tart 30
Old-fashioned Strawberry Shortcake 50
Palace Nut Cake 25   Assorted Cakes 30   French Pastry 20
Chocolate, Vanilla or Caramel Cup Custard 30

ICE CREAMS

Cup Lorraine 55   Pineapple Punch 45   Nelusko Parfait 45
Meringue Glace 45   Baked Alaska 65
Vanilla, Coffee, Chocolate, Pistachio or Strawberry 40
Loganberry, Raspberry, Strawberry, Orange or Lemon Water Ice 30

FRESH FRUITS

Pears 25   Grape Fruit 30   Strawberries, Raspberries or Blackberries 55 with Cream 65
Apple (1) 10   Orange (1) 15   Assorted Fruits 40
Watermelon 50

Guests are cordially invited to inspect our Kitchen, Pantries, etc.
Any Palace attendant will be pleased to show you through.

A 1925 menu includes the Green Goddess salad. (Palace Hotel)

The grand hotel continues to hold a place of honor at the center of San Francisco high society: The city's annual debutante ball, the Cotillion, has been held at the hotel – often in the Garden Court area – for more than a century. Holidays, especially Mother's Day, bring multiple generations of families to the Garden Court to celebrate together. "It's very typical to see four and five generations gather at these events," Roberts said.

IN THE CULINARY LANDSCAPE the Palace stakes a claim to the Green Goddess salad dressing, which Chef Philip Roemer is said to have invented in the 1920s in honor of actor George Arliss, who was staying at the hotel while performing in a play called The Green Goddess. Although the menu has evolved dramatically over the decades, diners can still enjoy a lunch on the menu since the early twentieth century: crab salad – now with a current version of the Green Goddess dressing.

The Palace is also renowned for its Manhattans. "Cocktail Bill" Boothby was something of a celebrity bartender when he started tending bar occasionally at the Palace soon after it reopened. Boothby had written the noted *Cocktail Boothby's American Bar-Tender* guide in 1891, and the Manhattan was his specialty. His Boothby Cocktail gave the classic a tweak: a champagne topper. (See the next chapter, on the House of Shields bar, for a recipe and more about Cocktail Boothby.)

Boothby held court in the Pied Piper Bar & Grill, named for the Maxfield Parrish "Pied Piper of Hamelin" mural that was commissioned for the hotel's reopening and, by popular demand, still hangs over the bar.

Parrish had previously painted "Old King Cole" for the Hotel Knickerbocker in New York. (That painting now hangs in the St. Regis Hotel bar in Manhattan.) In the "Pied Piper," Parrish himself is the face of the piper, his wife and mistress both appear in the painting, and two of the 27 children are based on Parrish's. The artist gave this advice to Palace bartenders: "When customers can no longer tell how many children they can count on the mural, send them home to their families."

Frederick Sharon paid $6,000 for the "Pied Piper" in 1909; today it would sell for between $5 million and $7 million.

In its lifetime, it's only left the bar three times. During Prohibition, when the bar was closed, the painting was moved to the hotel's Rose Room. During the 1989-1991 renovation, it was moved to the de Young Museum in Golden Gate Park. And in 2013, the "Pied Piper" was taken down and nearly sold. It likely would have left its bar home for good if not for the cries from dismayed citizens.

The Pied Piper mural has left the bar only three times – most recently in 2013, when it was nearly sold. Public outcry made the owners have a change of heart, and the painting was merely cleaned before returning to the bar. (Christopher Cellars, 2017)

That spring, the painting's sudden removal from the bar sparked loud protests from patrons, historians and politicians like Mayor Ed Lee. The hotel's owners were startled by the flood of protests and emails, and quickly canceled plans to sell the painting. "I don't think they realized how important it was to the city," Roberts said.

Instead of going to auction, the "Pied Piper" went to the cleaners. By August, it was restored to its lofty position above the bar. "People identify that painting with San Francisco," Mike Buhler of the group San Francisco Heritage told the *Chronicle*. "They have restored a small piece of the city's soul."

In its lifetime, the bar space has had a few different names and has been renovated, but it still has its original mosaic tile floor. In addition to its namesake mural, it features paintings by Antonio Sotomayor, who started as a dishwasher at the Palace after emigrating from Bolivia and eventually supervised all artistic endeavors at the hotel.

When asked how he felt about his art hanging in bars, Sotomayor responded: "Why paint if you don't want people to see it? Once we had churches, now we show our work in bars and restaurants."

So, for the price of a Boothby Cocktail – or even just a Coke – take a moment to soak up the fine art created just for the Palace's bar patrons and toast the San Franciscans who cared enough to save it.

2 New Montgomery St., between Market and Jessie streets
Phone: 415-512-1111
www.sfpalace.com

THE GREEN GODDESS

The china in this undated photo was the "gold service" commissioned for the Palace's reopening in 1909. (Palace Hotel)

THE PALACE HOTEL says the Green Goddess salad dressing was created in 1923 by Executive Chef Phillip Roemer. He came up with the dressing for a banquet honoring actor George Arliss, who was the lead in William Archer's hit play *The Green Goddess.* The dressing has evolved over the years.

1923: THE PALACE'S ORIGINAL GREEN GODDESS DRESSING

Ingredients:

- 1 cup mayonnaise
- 1/2 cup sour cream
- 1/4 cup snipped fresh chives or minced scallions
- 1/4 cup minced fresh parsley
- 1 tablespoon fresh lemon juice
- 1 tablespoon white wine vinegar
- 3 anchovy fillets, rinsed, patted dry, and minced
- Salt and freshly ground pepper to taste

Directions: Stir all the ingredients together in a small bowl until well blended. Taste and adjust the seasonings. Use immediately or cover and refrigerate. Yield: about 12 servings.

THE PALACE'S GREEN GODDESS DRESSING TODAY

Ingredients:

- 2 bunches of Italian flat leaf parsley (finely chopped)
- 2 bunches fresh chervil (finely chopped)
- 2 bunches tarragon (finely chopped)
- 5 cups fresh spinach
- 3 tablespoons chopped capers
- 1/2 cup chopped garlic
- 1/4 cup chopped shallots
- 1 tablespoon sugar
- 6 anchovies
- 3 cups tarragon vinegar (The Palace uses Beaufor vinegar imported from France)
- 1/2 cup Dijon mustard
- 3 egg yolks
- 6 cups corn oil

Directions: Place everything except oil in blender or in container and use emulsion blender. Blend on high until smooth, then while blending drizzle oil in mixture. Drizzle until oil is gone. Season with salt and pepper to taste. Yield: about 28 servings.

– Recipes courtesy of the Palace Hotel

WHAT WERE THEY EATING?

XMAS DINNER
PALACE HOTEL:
1910

(Palace Hotel)

The Palace Hotel has preserved a collection of menus going back more than 110 years, with at least one surviving from before the 1906 quake. Here are a few of the dishes that are hard to find in twenty-first century San Francisco:

1903: "BLOATER TOAST," 25 CENTS

Bloaters are lightly smoked, lightly salted herring that have not been gutted. Sometimes served chopped and sometimes ground into a paste, they often were eaten on toast with butter.

1903: "CHOW CHOW," 15 CENTS

Usually a relish of vegetables and pickles flavored with mustard. The dish is believed to have been brought to the United States by Chinese railroad laborers.

1910: "LUIZA TETRAZZINI," 60 CENTS

Paired with Mousse of Ham on the Christmas dinner menu, the baked-pasta dish typically combined strips of chicken with cooked spaghetti in a sherry-Parmesan cream sauce. Popular in the early twentieth century, the dish is named for opera singer Luisa Tetrazzini, who was beloved in San Francisco. In turn, she adored the city so much that she performed a free outdoor concert outside the Palace Hotel next to Lotta's Fountain on Christmas Eve, 1910.

1910: "NESSELRODE PUDDING," 35 CENTS

Named for a nineteenth-century Russian diplomat, the frozen dessert was a cream-enriched custard mixed with chestnut puree, candied fruits, currants, raisins, and maraschino liqueur.

– Sources: The Dictionary of Dainty Breakfasts (1899); The New Food Lover's Companion (2001); The San Francisco Call, Dec. 25, 1910

THE GENTLEMAN'S BAR

The House of Shields didn't start serving women until the 1970s, and didn't put stools along its bar rail until 1986. (House of Shields)

"Enter these portals and forget time and care."

– A sign, now gone, that for decades greeted visitors

to the House of Shields

The identity of this bartender sweeping up in the House of Shields sometime in the
mid-twentieth century is a mystery; the photo was passed along with the bar.
(House of Shields)

DIRECTLY ACROSS NEW MONTGOMERY STREET from the
Palace Hotel, the House of Shields bar has an overlapping history –
and occasionally a different spin on it.

The bar opened in 1912 on the ground floor of the new Sharon Building. The Sharon and the Palace were both owned by Frederick Sharon,
who hired George Kelham of New York as the post-earthquake architect
for the two properties. The *San Francisco Call* lauded the building plans in
1911: "This new office building will go a long way toward restoring the
prosperous conditions that existed in this busy south of Market district
before the fire."

Like most other San Francisco restaurants that opened in the chaotic
rebuilding period after the quake, details of the House of Shields' early
years are hazy, but former bar manager Eric Passetti has been piecing together stories behind the old bar since he helped restore it in 2010.

In March 1924, early in Prohibition, the Old Poodle Dog restaurant sign hangs on the east side of New Montgomery Street where the House of Shields is today. The bar was likely operating as a speakeasy in the basement. The Palace Hotel is across the street, on the left. (Bancroft Library photo, University of California, Berkeley)

For decades, the House of Shields has dated itself to 1908 – and its signs still say this. But Passetti discovered that the saloon on New Montgomery originally opened in 1912 under the name Grand Buffet. There was a House of Shields bar in California in 1908, he said – but in Montecito near Santa Barbara.

It was probably the late 1920s when a man named Eddie Shields, who had connections to the Santa Barbara area, took over the bar in the Sharon Building and renamed it the House of Shields.

Few records remain about Shields, who owned the bar for many years. A. William Smyth grew up with Shields' daughter decades later in Santa Barbara and said he had heard that in addition to running the bar, Shields was a horse-racing bookie who hung out with boxers like Jack Dempsey and organized Friday-night fights among inmates at Alcatraz. Shields also was said to be a bootlegger who ran liquor up the California coast from Mexico during Prohibition. An *Oakland Tribune* story from 1924 adds support to this part of the Shields story, reporting that a bootlegger named Eddie Shields was the target of an intended robbery after delivering liquor to a San Francisco apartment house. "He was a real scoundrel," said Smyth.

(Christopher Cellars, 2011)

Prohibition was widely flouted in San Francisco, where voters had overwhelmingly rejected a statewide version of the law, 104,817 to 22,024, and an official city police survey conducted in the early 1920s found 1,492 speakeasies in operation, despite the federal order. In 1926, the city's Board of Supervisors unanimously passed a resolution instructing the local police not to enforce Prohibition. Speakeasies had to operate under the table, but everyone knew they were there.

James Smith, author of *San Francisco's Lost Landmarks,* speculated that the bar in the House of Shields space simply moved downstairs to the basement of the Sharon Building during Prohibition. It's unclear whether the bar was still known as the Grand Buffet when Prohibition began.

A photograph of New Montgomery Street in 1924 shows a sign for the Old Poodle Dog restaurant where the House of Shields sign is today. City directories give a Sharon Building address for the Old Poodle Dog – a business that was a vocal opponent of Prohibition – and the restaurant apparently took over the prominent street-level space.

By the time Prohibition was repealed in 1933, the Sharon Building bar – possibly known by then as the House of Shields – had developed a reputation as a hangout for businessmen in the financial district. Stories from the time tell of a tunnel that once connected the Palace Hotel and the bar, allowing hotel guests to discreetly get to the bar for a drink. Passetti said he has found no evidence of such a tunnel, but points out old counters and other signs that a bar could have been operating for a time in the basement.

Urban legends swirl around the bar like the cigarette and pipe smoke that clouded the atmosphere for decades. One story has it that the long carved, mirrored back bar was originally made for the Palace Hotel, but that when the Maxfield Parrish mural was delivered to the hotel in 1909, it didn't leave room for the back bar so Frederick Sharon had it moved across the street. Passetti said he's inspected behind the bar in the House of Shields and he believes the story to be true. Although the Palace Hotel can't verify that this piece came from the hotel, they do say they have the front piece (where customers sit) of their original bar.

An old postcard advertising the House of Shields. (House of Shields)

Another historic point of contention: Some say that in 1923 President Harding died at the bar in the Sharon Building and had to be secretly carried across the street to his room at the Palace Hotel. Official accounts from the time report that the ailing president died in his suite at the Palace with his wife at his side.

With its original dark woodwork and warm, fluted-chandelier lighting – and its elaborate sconces dating to the 1930s – the House of Shields today still looks the part of the "gentlemen's club" that it was until 1972, when it finally started officially serving women. It was also the last bar in San Francisco to "sit down," adding stools along the rail only in 1986.

Passetti and the current owner, restaurateur Dennis Leary, took great care when they renovated the space. "Every single inch of the bar was refinished," Passetti said. "We didn't change anything; we just restored it."

A great deal of care went into the restoration of the House of Shields in 2010.
(Christopher Cellars, 2011)

San Francisco bars are in Passetti's DNA. After the 1906 earthquake, his great-grandfather ran a saloon called The Jolly Trio in North Beach – where his grandmother grew up down the street from Liguria Bakery – and his great-uncle owned the Gold Spike, a Columbus Avenue bar from the waning Barbary Coast days that lasted almost nine decades before closing in 2006. His grandfather also owned a North Beach bar, The M&B, in a space on Taylor now called Pat's Cafe, and Passetti grew up hearing stories about San Francisco's old bars and restaurants. Part of the bar his grandfather built is still in the cafe. "I stop into Pat's every once in a while to feel nostalgic."

Passetti has opened five bars in San Francisco and now owns the Old Ship Saloon, a location on Battery Street that has housed a bar since 1851 – the oldest bar address in the city. "I've kind of followed my history," he said.

When he was working with Leary to restore the House of Shields space, its past was top of mind. At first, the wood was so beaten up and dingy that the beauty in it was hard to see. But once the carved ceiling was cleaned and painted, Passetti saw the old bar's glory start to emerge. "Having respect for what it was originally intended for – that was my vision."

Old-timers still come in and tell tall tales about the bar and Eddie Shields, Passetti said: "People love making up stories about the House of Shields." These days on weekday evenings, the place is often packed with twenty-somethings meeting up for drinks. (No food is served in the bar.) "It's such a beautiful, unique space, and that's why people come."

For those who want to belly up to the bar and order a drink to toast its early days, Passetti said to keep in mind that a men's club in 1908 wouldn't have fussed much with cocktails.

His suggestion: a shot of whiskey and a beer.

39 New Montgomery St., between Market and Jessie streets
415-284-9958
www.thehouseofshields.com

THE LEGACY OF COCKTAIL BOOTHBY

WILLIAM T. BOOTHBY was born in San Francisco in 1862 and as a young man spent some time touring the West as a vaudevillian before he started mixing drinks at the city's bars in the 1880s. He published his first book in 1891, *Cocktail Boothby's American Bartender,* brimming with practical advice for nineteenth-century bartenders and saloon owners. Most of the copies of the original guide were destroyed in 1906; two are known to survive, and Anchor Distilling reprinted an edition in 2009.

After briefly serving as a California assemblyman, Boothby dedicated his second bartending guide, *The World's Drinks and How to Mix Them,* published in 1908, "to the liquor dealers of San Francisco, who unanimously assisted in my election to the legislature by an unprecedented majority."

Boothby tended bar at many saloons across the city, and some speculate he may have bartended under pseudonyms at times to avoid violating the barman's version of a "no-compete" clause. One of the bars he was best known for manning was at the Palace Hotel, starting soon after the quake. In 1934, four years after Boothby's death, the *San Francisco Recorder* reminisced:

> *"They were all aces at that mahogany, and Bill was the ace of aces. To see him rotating three cocktail glasses between the fingers of his left hand while measuring a jigger of gin or vermouth ... with the right was to witness a masterpiece of art in the making."*

Eric Passetti, owner of the Old Ship Saloon and former bar manager at the House of Shields, offers this recipe for the Boothby Cocktail, the famed bartender's twist on a Manhattan, invented at the Palace Hotel. Passetti also regularly featured the drink at the House of Shields. "I love to think that he came over here."

THE BOOTHBY MANHATTAN

Eric Passetti's Boothby Manhattan.
(Geri Migielicz, 2012)

Ingredients:
- Whiskey, 2/3 oz
- Italian vermouth, 1/3 oz
- Orange bitters, 2 dashes
- Angostura bitters, 2 drops
- Champagne, 1 bar spoon
- Cherry garnish

Directions: Shake whiskey, vermouth and bitters together with ice. Strain into a glass and top with Champagne. Garnish with a cherry.

– Source for Boothby biographical information: Cocktail Boothby's American Bartender, Anchor Distilling, 2009

THE AUTHOR'S HAUNT

John's Grill in Union Square has drawn politicians and other high-powered diners for more than a century. (Christopher Cellars, 2017)

"He went to John's Grill, asked the waiter to hurry his order of chops, baked potato, and sliced tomatoes, ate hurriedly, and was smoking a cigarette with his coffee when a thick-set youngish man with a plaid cap set askew above pale eyes and a tough cheery face came into the Grill and to his table. 'All set, Mr. Spade. She's full of gas and raring to go.'"
— The Maltese Falcon by Dashiell Hammett, published 1930

John's Grill was already open on the right side of this block of Ellis Street when this photo was taken about 1909 – around the time the city started lobbying to host the 1915 Panama-Pacific International Exposition. The photo is taken from Powell Street, looking east to Market Street. (San Francisco History Center, San Francisco Public Library)

DASHIELL HAMMETT STARTED DINING – and undoubtedly drinking – at John's Grill soon after he first came to San Francisco in the early 1920s. The aspiring young writer worked as an operative for the Pinkerton National Detective Agency in the Flood Building next door, and despite Prohibition, booze was said to be had for patrons who went upstairs by the side entrance.

The city was just 15 years removed from the quake when Hammett arrived, and his new hangout had played a role in the business district's recovery, claiming the distinction of being the first restaurant to open in the rebuilt downtown core. Plans for the restaurant had actually been in the works before the quake struck, and in 1908, Wilfrid Girard opened John's Grill on Ellis Street, even though his business partner, John Monaco, had died – reportedly in a cable car accident.

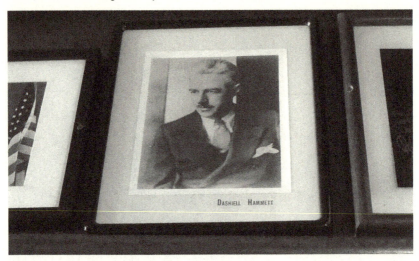

Dashiell Hammett's picture is one of many famous portraits adorning the walls. (Christopher Cellars, 2017)

By the time Hammett settled in at John's Grill with his "coffee" and cigarettes, Girard was also running Girard's French Restaurant upstairs, where his staff created a salad dressing that eventually was sold nationally. Girard owned John's Grill until 1954, and over the decades the restaurant tucked around the corner from Market Street became a destination for the politicians and celebrities whose portraits line the walls.

Politicians and business executives still hold high-powered meetings at the white-clothed tables, and the rule is that if your picture is on the wall, you sit under your own mug. The current owner, appropriately named John Konstin, also hosts an Election Day lunch well-attended by the state's political elite.

Konstin's father, Gus, bought John's Grill in the 1960s, and Konstin got an early education in the restaurant business: "Since I was a little kid, I was here washing dishes." His son finished culinary school in summer 2017 and is preparing to be the third generation of the Konstin family to run the landmark restaurant.

John Konstin says a key to the family's business survival was the foresight his mother, Sydna, had to purchase the building in the 1970s. "We had to sell four buildings to buy this building."

His parents thoroughly embraced the Hammett legacy, and Konstin keeps it alive. Although the restaurant itself does not make a cameo in the 1941 film of *The Maltese Falcon*, the movie is a star at John's Grill. On the second floor landing, a replica of the black bird figure used in the movie sits under a spotlight – and lock and key after an earlier replica was stolen in 2007. Humphrey Bogart, Mary Astor, Peter Lorre and Sydney Greenstreet gaze out at fans from movie scenes on the walls of the second and third floor dining rooms.

An elevator was added in 2017, but John's Grill maintains a dark-wood look reminiscent of its early days. Konstin says the layout of the first floor is much the same as it was when it opened in 1908, and the restaurant's retro vibe continues to draw a healthy mix of locals and tourists. He has no plans to make any cosmetic updates: "Why would we modernize and look like everyone else?"

(Christopher Cellars, 2012)

And Sam Spade's lamb chops with baked potato and sliced tomatoes are still featured on the menu for a power lunch or a dinner accompanied by the nightly live jazz. But don't be like Spade and rush through the chops: Order an Anchor Steam beer, served in the city since 1896, and take your time savoring San Francisco's classics.

63 Ellis St.
415-986-3274
www.johnsgrill.com

CHEERS TO THE BON VIVANTS

An undated illustration of Schroeder's shows the men of the Financial District enjoying the restaurant's hearty food and beer. (Schroeder's)

"His unpretentious café on Pine street drew its patronage from merchants of the wholesale district, bankers and brokers from the financial district, politicians, sportsmen, theatrical folk and bon vivants from various walks of life."

– San Franciso Chronicle, July 5, 1921

Schroeder's returned to the Financial District within a couple of years of the quake. This is the cafe in 1935, before the murals were painted. (Schroeder's)

WALK INTO SCHROEDER'S on a weekday afternoon, and you'll see the denizens of the Financial District throughout – men and women in suits tucked in with cocktails at the bar, and long blond-wood tables full of chatty workmates nursing foamy pints.

In spirit – if not location – Schroeder's is the same as it was before the 1906 earthquake.

Since its earliest days, Schroeder's has been known as a place for businesspeople to rendezvous over German beer and hearty food. Henry Schroeder of Hamburg, Germany, was 30 when he opened his restaurant in 1893 at the corner of Market and Pine streets just a couple of blocks from where Schroeder's is today.

The *San Francisco Chronicle* called Schroeder's "a place to seek": "His unpretentious café on Pine street drew its patronage from merchants of the wholesale district, bankers and brokers from the financial district, politicians, sportsmen, theatrical folk and bon vivants from various walks of life."

Henry Schroeder,
Chronicle obituary photo

After the quake, Schroeder was forced to move the restaurant out to the Mission neighborhood for a time, but he remained committed to the Financial District and was active in recovery efforts there. By 1907, he had already secured a new home for the restaurant at 117 Front Street, and may have relocated the café there as quickly as the next year. He tried out at least a couple of locations on Front Street over the next 12 years.

When Schroeder died after a short illness in 1921, The *Chronicle* noted, "Many prominent persons of San Francisco were his friends and he was noted for his liberality and good humor as well as for the excellence of the viands he served."

The news of Schroeder's death reached Germany, where another German transplant to San Francisco, T. Max Kniesche, was visiting family. Kniesche had never been inside the restaurant, but he knew he wanted to buy it.

Kniesche had first arrived in San Francisco in late summer 1907 when many quake refugees were still sleeping in parks. In an interview with a University of California, Berkeley, historian nearly 70 years later, he described a burned-out city still cleaning up: "I'll tell you what you saw on the streets when you stood down below the Ferry Building, and you looked up through the city. It looked like it would be a harbor there, but nothing but masts standing there. All that was left was the smokestacks. It looked just like it would be a fleet there."

Kniesche worked in several restaurants as the city recovered. In 1921, he had lost a lot of money in a business deal, so he and his wife returned to Germany while he contemplated moving to South America. Getting word that Schroeder's owner had died changed those plans. "I just had enough money to buy the place. I never looked at it, never looked in, never been inside of it. I just knew a fellow who worked there, and he told me about it, and said it look good."

After Prohibition ended, Schroeder's was open to women – but for dinner hours only.
The lunch hour was closed to women until 1970. (Schroeder's, undated)

In 1922, early in the Prohibition era, Kniesche bought a beer hall that couldn't serve beer. He fixed up the place "German-style" and for more than a decade it was primarily a lunch spot that was open only to men. After Prohibition ended and beer service was restored, Kniesche expanded to dinner, and women were allowed into Schroeder's for the first time – but only for dinner. Women were not welcome in the restaurant during the busy lunch hours until 1970.

The restaurant focused on traditional hearty German food and beer, and sauerbraten with potato pancakes was the most popular dish for decades.

The décor was plain at first, but in 1939 – the year of the Golden Gate International Exposition on Treasure Island – an artist from Hamburg named Herman Richter walked into the restaurant and offered to paint scenes in exchange for food and drink. It took Richter about a year to complete about 17 oil paintings. After Kniesche moved the café to its current location on Front Street in 1956, he hired artist Donat Ivanovsky to paint three more to finish out the décor. "They cost me more than the whole bunch of original ones put together," he remembered years later.

This photograph from 1924 shows the block on Front Street between Sacramento and California streets where Schroeder's moved in 1956. Schroeder's still thrives in this location. (San Francisco History Center, San Francisco Public Library)

The paintings still set the mood at Schroeder's – along with taxidermy and a collection of steins that Kniesche started. The rosewood back bar still in the café was believed to have arrived in San Francisco by ship in the late 1880s.

Kniesche died in 1985 and his family kept Schroeder's until 1990. Jana and Stefan Filipcik purchased the restaurant in 1997 and nurtured the beer hall's tradition as a lively meeting spot for local workers for more than 15 years.

Two of the twentysomething workers commiserating over beers at Schroeder's in the early 2000s were college friends Jan Wiginton and Andy Chun. Wiginton had studied in Austria, and she had an affinity for the German food and atmosphere. "I loved the beer hall culture."

At the time, Wiginton was working in the tech industry and Chun worked in private equity. They made the leap to restaurant ownership in 2008 with Press Club, a stylish wine bar near the Moscone Center.

Schroeder's still showcases many of the murals and steins that were collected over the decades. (Schroeder's)

As they mulled over their next venture, they knew they wanted it to involve an existing space, rather than starting from scratch. Then, in 2013, they learned Schroeder's was for sale. "I thought, 'This is a gift!' " Wiginton says. "We should save Schroeder's!"

The partners were committed to the old-school vibe, but knew the look needed some 21st-century updates. "In my mind, Schroeder's was a diamond in the rough," Wiginton says. They worked with the building owner in changing the façade, opening up the front of the 200-plus-seat space and bringing in more modern furniture, but it was important to them to keep the murals, the light fixtures and the steins – touches that keep Schroeder's connected to its past.

And while the time-intensive sauerbraten is now considered a special-occasion dish rather than a regular feature, the menu still focuses on hearty German fare like bratwurst and Wiener schnitzel, which are customers' current favorites. Schroeder's also offers the opportunity to compare flights of German and American beers, or to explore the world of schnapps.

A detail from one of the murals. (Christopher Cellars, 2011)

Wiginton and Chun now own a total of four locations downtown, including the Elite Café and Pacific Cocktail Haven, but Schroeder's holds a special place in their hearts. "We are part of a long line of people who have held it for a period of time," Wiginton says. "We look at ourselves as stewards."

240 Front St.
415-421-4778
www.schroederssf.com

OTHER TABLES AROUND TOWN

The Buena Vista Cafe opened in 1891 and moved to its current location in 1916.
(Buena Vista Cafe)

There are many more restaurants around the city where diners can get a taste of the San Francisco that emerged after the 1906 quake. Here are a few other destinations that opened or reopened in the recovery years after the quake, leading up to the 1915 Panama-Pacific International Exposition. All are worth a stop in a continuing exploration of the city's rich culinary history.

(Restaurants and bars are listed starting with locations at the north tip of the city and moving generally clockwise.)

(Tandemvines Media, 2011)

THE BUENA VISTA CAFE, FISHERMAN'S WHARF

2765 Hyde St. Phone: 415-474-5044
www.thebuenavista.com

Best known as the place that brought Irish coffee to America, The Buena Vista Café's roots go back to 1891, when it opened about a block away from its current location. The BV, as locals call it, moved to the corner of Beach and Hyde in 1916, a year after the Panama-Pacific International Exposition. The BV was popular among fishermen and workers at the nearby sardine cannery.

The official story is that the building above the cafe was originally a boardinghouse, but some in the neighborhood say the building once housed a brothel and that's why the women's restrooms are upstairs and the men's restrooms are downstairs. The Irish coffee – still made using the 1952 recipe – definitely makes it worth a stop. And for a uniquely San Francisco treat: Take the Powell and Hyde cable car directly to the BV from Union Square.

THE SALOON, NORTH BEACH

1232 Grant Ave. Phone: 415-989-7666
www.sfblues.weebly.com

The Saloon opened as early as 1861 and was known in the 1860s as Wagner's Beer Hall, according to water permits from the time. Drunken sailors leaving the bar were in danger of getting shanghaied in the city's wild Barbary Coast days. The story goes that the building survived the 1906 quake because of its exceptionally sturdy timbers and escaped the fires because the brothel upstairs was a favorite of the city's firemen. Today, the Saloon still looks the part of its rough-and-tumble past with its worn wood bar and cheap drinks. It's a destination for dedicated blues fans, who enjoy live music every night.

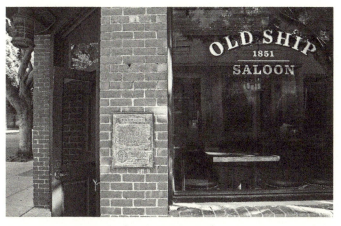

(Jessica Stout, 2017)

THE OLD SHIP SALOON, JACKSON SQUARE

298 Pacific Ave. Phone: 415-788-2222
www.theoldshipsf.com

The Old Ship Saloon is a survivor from the city's earliest days. It opened in 1851 in the hull of the Arkansas, a ship that ran aground at Bird Island (Alcatraz) and was towed to shore. Ships were regularly abandoned at the time as prospectors dashed off to the gold mines, and the wrecked Arkansas' hull quickly housed a saloon. Although the ship is long gone, a bar has stood there ever since. It's had a few names in its lifetime – such as Babe's Monte Carlo and Bricks – but since 1992 it's been known as the Old Ship Saloon.

The Old Ship was purchased in 2017 by owners dedicated to the neighborhood's history, including Eric Passetti, who was manager during the renovation at the House of Shields. Passetti has maintained the neighborhood bar vibe and draws inspiration from his own Barbary Coast ancestry: His great-uncle was a bartender on Pacific Avenue in the early 1900s. "It feels good to carry a torch and be a custodian of someplace that's been here for so long."

TADICH GRILL, FINANCIAL DISTRICT
240 California St. Phone: 415-391-1849
www.tadichgrill.com

Every San Franciscan who has learned about this journey has asked, "Are you going to Tadich?"

Tadich Grill has the honor of being the oldest restaurant in the state. It was first opened by Croatian immigrants as "Coffee Stand" on the city's wharf in 1849, the boom year of the California Gold Rush. The restaurant has moved several times around the then-waterfront that is now the Financial District, before and since the 1906 earthquake. John Tadich began working at the restaurant as a bartender in the 1870s and bought it in 1887, and it was after the quake that the restaurant became the Tadich Grill. The Buich brothers started working at Tadich in 1913 and 1914, and bought the restaurant in 1928. The Buich family moved the restaurant to the current location on California Street in the late 1960s, and still owns the San Francisco classic today.

The long wooden bar is always packed and Tadich doesn't take reservations, but it's worth the wait to get a seat. Once there, it's the perfect place to enjoy a Crab Louie, a dish some claim was created in San Francisco around 1910, or the Hangtown Fry, the omelet of oysters, eggs and bacon that was said to be created in the Gold Rush town of Placerville for gold miners who could afford the pricey ingredients. It has been on the Tadich menu for generations, likely in some form since the late 1800s.

SAM'S GRILL, FINANCIAL DISTRICT
374 Bush St. Phone: 415-421-0594
www.samsgrillsf.com/

Sam's Grill opened first as an oyster saloon in an open-air food market on California Street in 1867. The owner, Irish immigrant Michael Molan Moraghan, also farmed oysters on thousands of acres of tideflats in the bay and Moraghan was known as the "Oyster King." After the quake, Moraghan moved his oyster business around a few different locations in the city. In 1919, he brought the business – then called the Burlingame Oyster Company – into a rebuilt California Market between California and Pine streets on Montgomery. In 1922, Sam Zenovich bought the company. It had a few different names before settling on Sam's Seafood Grotto in 1931. In 1937, the next owner, Frank Zeput, made it officially Sam's Grill, and after World War II, the restaurant moved to its current location.

In 2014, the restaurant closed for a few months and the Financial District regulars feared that was the end of the classic seafood house. But some of the loyal customers came up with a plan to save it, reopening that fall. In 2015, Sam's added a patio space, so its fresh shucked oysters can be savored in the fresh air, just like in the old days.

ST. FRANCIS HOTEL, UNION SQUARE
335 Powell St. Phone: 415-397-7000
www.westinstfrancis.com

Inspired by San Francisco's desire to be the "Paris of the West," the St. Francis Hotel was built in the image of the grand hotels of Europe. The chef at the 1904 opening was Victor Hirtzler, who came from Strasbourg via New York. In 1906, the hotel suffered some damage in the quake, but Hirtzler still managed to open for breakfast, serving diners including opera singer Enrico Caruso, who came over from the Palace Hotel. Later that day, the fires engulfing the city scorched the St. Francis, and refugees from the hotel set up camp in Union Square. They were served meals by hotel cooks and the square earned the nickname "Little St. Francis." The next year, the hotel reopened. Decades later, the hotel hosted earthquake survivors for a "survivors' breakfast" each year on the anniversary of the quake, featuring versions of the menu of April 18, 1906: chilled rhubarb stew, southern hominy with cream, and eggs with black truffles in puff pastry.

Today, the Clock Bar off the lobby embraces the hotel's past with rotating menus that explore time periods like the hotel's Gilded Age heyday. The Oak Room Restaurant still has the wood paneling from 1913, when it opened as the Men's Bar. After dinner or a drink, explore the historic photos and menus showcased in the lobby.

(Tandemvines Media, 2013)

THE HOTEL UTAH SALOON, SOUTH OF MARKET

500 Fourth St. 415-546-6300

www.hotelutah.com/

The Deininger family opened the Hotel Utah Saloon in 1908 in the South of Market neighborhood, a working-class section of the city that had been razed by the fires after the earthquake. The Deiningers ordered the saloon's ornate back bar from Belgium and served Fredericksburg beer, which the bar called the best beer in the city.

The completion of the Bay Bridge in 1936 brought a wave of long-shoremen and merchants to the saloon and hotel. In the 1950s, the bar was run by Al Opatz, who was famous for cutting ties off unsuspecting overdressed patrons. The stage was built in the 1970s by the next owner, Paul Gaer, who co-wrote the Robert Redford film The Electric Horseman.

Now in a neighborhood remade by the arrival of several tech companies, the Utah continues to serve up classic beers at the long wood bar, and its stage features live music most nights.

Red's Java House in 2011, left, and the other Java House in 2016. (Tandemvines Media)

THE TWO JAVA HOUSES, THE EMBARCADERO
Red's Java House

Pier 30. 415-777-5626

www.redsjavahouse.com

The Java House

Pier 40. 415-495-7260

www.javahousesf.com/

Red's Java House has been a bit more in the spotlight in recent years – getting notice for its hearty breakfasts from food celebrities like Anthony Bourdain – but it's the Java House farther south on the Embarcadero that came first, dating to the post-earthquake recovery years.

When the Java House opened in 1912, the waterfront was bustling with construction, and the wharf shack served hot dogs and coffee to longshoremen, sailors and dock workers. In the 1950s, a redhead named Mike McGarvey bought the Java House and ran it with his brother, Tom. The brothers eventually sold the Java House and bought a joint called Franco's Lunch at Pier 30. Franco's Lunch had served a similar waterfront clientele since the 1930s, and the brothers renamed it Red's Java House.

The original Java House went through a few more owners before it was bought by Philip and Sotiria Papadopoulos in 1983. Their family continues to run the restaurant today.

Both Java Houses still serve solid dockworkers' fare, leaning heavily on hearty egg breakfasts, as well as burgers and hot dogs – all best washed down with a beer.

(Darren Edwards, The Elixir, 2017)

THE ELIXIR, MISSION DISTRICT

3200 16th St. 415-552-1633
www.facebook.com/elixirsaloon/

Owners of the Elixir say a bar has been standing on the corner of 16th and Guerrero streets since 1858. At the time of the earthquake, a lawyer named Patrick McGinnis owned the bar, and he rebuilt it within a year or so on the same spot. During Prohibition, the bar was run as a "soft drink parlor." Through the next several decades, the bar had several names – the Hunt-In Club, Swede's, Club Corona – before becoming Jack's Elixir Bar in the late 1990s. The current owners renovated the bar in 2003 and fully embraced the cocktail culture sweeping the city. The Elixir has landed on many best-bars lists in recent years.

THE OLD CLAM HOUSE, BAYVIEW

299 Bayshore Blvd. 415-826-4880
www.theoldclamhousesf.com/

Opened as the Oakdale Bar and Clam House in 1861, the Clam House holds the distinction of being the city's oldest restaurant in its original location. When it was opened by Ambrose and Anna Zurfluh, the restaurant was on the waterfront, but the bay around it was gradually filled in. In its early years, a two-mile plank road linked the neighborhood to downtown San Francisco. The 1906 fires stopped short of the restaurant, and today, the 1861 building survives to house the bar section.

The specialty when it opened was clams and oysters from the bay. While the San Francisco Bay fisheries have long been depleted, diners can still savor a shellfish feast that looks and tastes like a sizzling blast from the past: clams, mussels, crab and shrimp roasted on a cast-iron skillet.

(Christopher Cellars, 2011)

CLIFF HOUSE, OCEAN BEACH
1090 Point Lobos. Phone: 415-386-3330
www.cliffhouse.com

This storied restaurant's history goes back to 1863. It survived the 1906 earthquake only to burn down a year later, and it has been reincarnated again and again through several renovations. (The website has an extensive illustrated timeline on the restaurant's evolution over the past 150-plus years.) It is still in the same glorious location overlooking the Pacific Ocean — a beautiful spot for a sunset dinner.

ACKNOWLEDGEMENTS

THE STORIES BEHIND RESTAURANTS are often the stories of hard-working people who start and end their days in the wee hours of the morning. I am grateful for these big-hearted folks who take time to tell their stories in between cutting up fish, maneuvering hot pans of focaccia, steaming rice noodles, and serving long lines of customers.

I owe three harmonies of thanks to Julie and David Ho, who have generously – and regularly – shared their story with me for more than five years.

Thank you to the Sancimino and Soracco families for welcoming me behind the scenes at their busy restaurants, and to Michael La Rocca for his tales of the "Crab King." Thanks to John Konstin and Jonny Raglin for their time and insights. and to Renée Roberts for her assistance in the research of the Palace Hotel. Extra appreciation goes to Eric Passetti, whose passion for San Francisco's rich restaurant and bar history is boundless.

I am grateful for research guidance from Susan Goldstein, city archivist at the San Francisco Public Library's History Center, who also graciously vetted the introduction. Thanks to James R. Smith, author of San Francisco's Lost Landmarks, and Charlie Chin, artist in residence at the Chinese Historical Society of America, for sharing their expertise. Thanks to the photo librarians who patiently answered questions: Susan Snyder at The Bancroft Library, University of California, Berkeley; Christina Moretta at the San Francisco Historical Photograph Collection, San Francisco Public Library; Kathleen Correia in the California History Section, California State Library, and Mary Morganti at the California Historical Society.

A long-overdue Boothby Manhattan to Heidi de Laubenfels, who has cheered me on from the earliest days of this project.

A toast to Geri Migielicz, whose videos brought the stories to life in the multimedia iBook edition. And a round to Kris Higginson, whose careful editing made the text shine. Many thanks to Suki Dardarian, Leon Espino-za, Kathleen Triesch Saul, Whitney Stensrud, and others in my extended Seattle Times family who encouraged my work on this story.

I am forever grateful for the friends like Hon Walker and Catherine Hawley who urged me to take the leap necessary to do this project – and especially to Gretchen Bay and Sutton Long, who have again and again hosted me in their beautiful home. I owe you a lifetime supply of Liguria Bakery focaccia.

To my mom, who is understandably amused that the child who was such a picky eater grew into a woman who waxes poetic over raw oysters: Thank you for instilling in me a love for good stories and for encouraging me to tell them. To my dad, who would have enjoyed shooting the breeze with the fellows at Swan, I owe my deep appreciation for hard work – both others' and my own.

And to Chris, my partner in love, good food and all of life: I am in awe of what we've been able to do together so far. I can't wait to start our next adventure.

PHOTOGRAPHY

HISTORIC PHOTOGRAPHY

Thank you to the following libraries and archives, which provided photo-research guidance and granted permission to publish historic images from the years after the 1906 earthquake.

California State Library, Sacramento, California: library.ca.gov
California Historical Society: californiahistoricalsociety.org
The Bancroft Library, University of California, Berkeley: bancroft.berkeley.edu
Chinese Historical Society of America: chsa.org
Library of Congress: loc.gov/pictures
San Francisco History Center, San Francisco Public Library: sfpl.org
U.S. Geological Survey: libraryphoto.cr.usgs.gov

RECENT PHOTOGRAPHY

Most of the current photographs were shot by Christopher Cellars and Denise Clifton for Tandemvines Media. Many thanks to the restaurants that granted use of their images in this book, as well as Geri Migielicz of Story4. Credits are included with each image.

BIBLIOGRAPHY

BOOKS
Sources on historic San Francisco and its restaurants

Frances deTalavera Berger and John Parke Custis, *Sumptuous Dining in Gaslight San Francisco: 1875-1915* (New York: Doubleday, 1985).

William T. (Cocktail) Boothby, *The World's Drinks and How to Mix Them* (San Francisco, Calif.: Pacific Buffet, Pacific Building, 1908).

Jane Chamberlin and Hank Armstrong, *The Great and Notorious Saloons of San Francisco* (Santa Barbara, Calif.: Capra Press, 1982).

Andrea Rees Davies, *Saving San Francisco: Relief and Recovery After the 1906 Disaster* (Philadelphia, Pa.: Temple University Press, 2011).

Philip L. Fradkin, *The Great Earthquake and Firestorms of 1906: How San Francisco Nearly Destroyed Itself* (Berkeley and Los Angeles, Calif.: University of California Press, 2005).

Philip L. Fradkin, *Magnitude 8: Earthquakes and Life Along the San Andreas Fault* (New York: Henry Holt and Co., 1998).

George Kao, *Cathay By the Bay: San Francisco Chinatown in 1950* (Hong Kong: The Chinese University Press, 1988).

Oscar Lewis and Carroll D. Hall, *Bonanza Inn: America's First Luxury Hotel (New York: Alfred A. Knopf Inc., 7th Printing, 1949).*

Fritz Maytag and David Burkhart, foreword to *Cocktail Boothby's American Bartender,* by William T. Boothby (San Francisco, Calif.: New Anchor Distilling Edition, 2009).

Duggan McDonnell, *Drinking the Devil's Acre: A Love Letter from San Francisco and Her Cocktails* (San Francisco, Calif.: Chronicle Books, 2015).

Leta E. Miller, *Music and Politics in San Francisco: From the 1906 Quake to the Second World War* (Berkeley and Los Angeles, Calif: University of California Press, 2011).

Doris Muscatine, *A Cook's Tour of San Francisco* (New York: Charles Scribner's Sons, 1963).

The Refugees' Cook Book (The 1906 San Francisco Earthquake and Fire Digital Collection, The Bancroft Library, University of California, Berkeley), accessed June 22, 2012, http://content.cdlib.org/ark:/13030/hb7q2nb55j/?order=3&brand=calisphere

James R. Smith, *San Francisco's Lost Landmarks* (Fresno, Calif.: Craven Street Books, 2005), especially Ch. 9.

Rebecca Solnit, *A Paradise Built in Hell* (New York: Viking Penguin, 2009), especially 13-33.

Rufus Steele, *The City That Is: The Story of the Rebuilding of San Francisco in Three Years* (San Francisco, Calif.: A.M. Robertson, 1909), especially Kindle edition, 219.

Stephen Tobriner, *Bracing for Disaster: Earthquake-Resistant Architecture and Engineering in San Francisco, 1838-1933* (Berkeley, Calif.: Heyday Books, 2006).

Ruth Thompson and Louis Hanges, *Eating Around San Francisco* (Los Angeles and San Francisco, Calif.: Suttonhouse, 1937).

Clifford James Walker, *One Eye Closed, The Other Red: The California Bootlegging Years* (Barstow, Calif.: Back Door Publishing, 1999).

Evelyn Wells, *Champagne Days of San Francisco* (New York: Appleton Century, 1939).

Sources on food

Phillis Browne, *The Dictionary of Dainty Breakfasts* (London: Cassell, 1899), accessed June 22, 2012, through Google Books. https://books.google.com/books?id=Al0EAAAAYAAJ&printsec=frontcover&source=gbs_ge_summary_r&cad=0%23v=onepage&q&f=false#v=onepage&q&f=false

Carol Field, *The Italian Baker* (Berkeley, Calif.: Ten Speed Press, 2011).

Marcella Hazan, Essentials of Classic Italian Cooking (New York: A.A. Knopf, 2008).

Sharon Tyler Herbst, *The New Food Lover's Companion* (New York: Barron's Educational Services, 2001).

Evan Jones, "Delmonico's," in *Not for Bread Alone: Writers on Food, Wine, and the Art of Eating,* ed. Dan Halpern (New York: Harper Perennial, 2008).

JOURNALS AND ARTICLES

Simon Baker, "San Francisco in Ruins: The 1906 Aerial Photographs of George R. Lawrence," *Landscape* Vol. 30, No. 2 (1989): 9-14.

Will Irwin, "The City That Was," *The (New York) Sun*, April 21, 1906.

James Oseland, "Local Favorite," *Saveur*, December 2011, 63.

"Native Oysters Are Small, But Sweet," *San Francisco Call*, April 20, 1909, 10.

Coverage of Lawsuit Against Accursio La Rocca, *San Francisco Chronicle*, December 3-18, 1918, multiple pages.

"Jim Griffin, Noted Fight Referee, Dies," *San Francisco Chronicle*, September 10, 1935, 13.

"Obituaries: Girard, Restaurant Operator," *San Francisco Examiner*, September 20, 1962, 19.

"Henry Schroeder, Known to Local Bon Vivants, Dies," *San Francisco Chronicle*, July 5, 1921, 20.

ONLINE SOURCES

"The Bancroft Library Presents The 1906 San Francisco Earthquake and Fire," University of California, Berkeley, accessed April, May, and June, 2012. http://bancroft.berkeley.edu/collections/earthquakeandfire/index2.html
Notably, these sections:

"Report of Dr. Edward T. Devine to Hon. William H. Taft, President, American National Red Cross, Washington, D.C."

Sunset magazine's earthquake-related issues.

Operation Kaleidoscope: Melange of Personal Recollections: "A City in Ruins."

"The Great Quake, 1906-2006," Centennial coverage by the *San Francisco Chronicle*, April 9-18, 2006. Accessed May-June 2012. Especially the following:

Karola Saekel, "Quake Cuisine," April 12, 2006. http://www.sfgate.com/default/article/The-Great-Quake-1906-2006-Quake-cuisine-2520098.php

Carl Nolte, "The Refugees," April 14, 2006. http://www.sfgate.com/default/article/The-Great-Quake-1906-2006-The-Refugees-2537336.php#page-2

Carl Nolte, "The Last Stand," April 15, 2006. http://www.sfgate.com/default/article/The-Great-Quake-1906-2006-The-last-stand-2537403.php

Carl Nolte, "A Great City Reduced to Rubble," April 16, 2006. http://www.sfgate.com/default/article/The-Great-Quake-1906-2006-A-great-city-reduced-2520210.php

Patricia Yollin, "Earthquake Diaries: Carrie Mangels, Elsie Cross," April 16, 2006. http://www.sfgate.com/default/article/The-Great-Quake-1906-2006-Earthquake-diaries-2519888.php

Carl Nolte, "From Smoke and Ruin, a New City," April 18, 2006. http://www.sfgate.com/default/article/The-Great-Quake-1906-2006-From-smoke-and-ruin-2537180.php

Carl Nolte, "Rising from the Ashes," April 18, 2006.
http://www.sfgate.com/default/article/The-Great-Quake-1906-2006-Rising-from-the-ashes-2537103.php

The San Francisco Call, 1906-1915, Library of Congress, Chronicling America, accessed May and June, 2012, http://chroniclingamerica.loc.gov/

"1906 Earthquake: Refugee Camps," National Park Service, Presidio of San Francisco, accessed June 11, 2012, http://www.nps.gov/prsf/historyculture/1906-earthquake-relief-efforts-living-accommodations.htm

"A Great Civic Drama," The Virtual Museum of the City of San Francisco, accessed June 11, 2012, http://www.sfmuseum.org/hist/timeline.html

"Timeline of Italian Americans in California," The Bancroft Library, University of California, Berkeley, accessed June 2012, http://bancroft.berkeley.edu/collections/italianamericans/timeline_immigration.html

James R. Smith, "PPIE: San Francisco's Finest World Fair (Part 2)," Guidelines, San Francisco City Guides, accessed June 12, 2012, http://www.sfcityguides.org/public_guidelines.html?article=515&submitted=TRUE&srch_text=&submitted2=&topic=Events

"History," Fior d'Italia website, accessed May 2012. (Note: website closed after restaurant couldn't reopen.)

"History," Tadich Grill, accessed June 20, 2012, http://www.tadichgrill.com/history.php

San Francisco city directories (multiple years), Internet Archive, http://archive.org/search.php?query=san%20francisco%20city%20directory%20AND%20mediatype%3Atexts

"Enrico Caruso and the San Francisco Earthquake," The Virtual Museum of the City of San Francisco, accessed June 20, 2012, http://www.sfmuseum.org/1906/ew19.html

"History, Palace Hotel, a Luxury Collection Hotel," Historic Hotels of America, accessed June 20, 2012, and May 13, 2017, http://www.historichotels.org/hotels-resorts/palace-hotel/history.php

"History," Palace Hotel, accessed June 20, 2012, http://www.sfpalace.com/history

George Kelham biography, Pacific Coast Architecture Database, University of Washington, accessed June 20, 2012, http://pcad.lib.washington.edu/person/294/

Lynne Charr Bennett, "Swan Oyster Depot Endures," *San Francisco Chronicle*, December 11, 2011, accessed August/September 2017, http://www.sfgate.com/food/article/Swan-Oyster-Depot-endures-2393125.php

Carl Nolte, "Restored Pied Piper Returns to Namesake Bar," *San Francisco Chronicle*, August 23, 2013, accessed May 13, 2017, http://www.sfgate.com/bayarea/article/Restored-Pied-Piper-returns-to-namesake-bar-4754251.php

John Coté, "John's Grill Marks Its Centennial," *San Francisco Chronicle*, December 21, 2008, accessed August 2017, http://www.sfgate.com/restaurants/article/John-s-Grill-marks-its-centennial-3257300.php

Kniesche, T. Max. "Schroeder's Café and the German Restaurant Tradition in San Francisco, 1907-1976." Interview by Ruth Teiser, Oral History Center, Bancroft Library, University of California, Berkeley, accessed May and August, 2017, https://archive.org/details/schroederscafeger00knierich

Paolo Lucchesi, "San Francisco Institution Schroeder's Readies For New Owners, New Era," *San Francisco Chronicle*, accessed May and August 2017, http://insidescoopsf.sfgate.com/blog/2013/11/27/san-francisco-institution-schroeders-readies-for-new-owners-new-era/

Ellen Huet, "The Saloon, S.F.'s Oldest Bar and Live Blues Venue Turns 150 This Weekend," *SF Weekly*, October 7, 2011, accessed August 2017, https://archives.sfweekly.com/shookdown/2011/10/07/the-saloon-sfs-oldest-bar-and-live-blues-venue-turns-150-this-weekend

Amanda Gold, "Bay Area Stars Freshening Up 5 Classic Dishes," *San Francisco Chronicle*, May 31, 2009, accessed August 2017, http://www.sfgate.com/food/article/Bay-Area-stars-freshening-up-5-classic-dishes-3296739.php

Paolo Lucchesi, "Sam's Grill To Reopen, Refurbished By Its Faithful," *San Francisco Chronicle*, September 3, 2014, accessed August 2017, http://www.sfgate.com/insidescoop/article/Sam-s-Grill-to-reopen-refurbished-by-its-faithful-5732211.php

Paolo Lucchesi, "Port History: Java House on Pier 40," *San Francisco Chronicle*, October 22, 2013, accessed August 2017, http://insidescoopsf.sfgate.com/blog/2013/10/22/port-history-java-house-on-pier-40/

Allen Matthews, "Red's Java House – San Francisco Waterfront Classic,"
    San Francisco Chronicle, September 20, 2013, accessed August 2017, http://
    www.sfgate.com/restaurants/article/Red-s-Java-House-San-Francisco-
    waterfront-4721347.php
"The Story of Sam Wo Restaurant in San Francisco Chinatown," Sky Link TV,
    August 31, 2017, accessed September 14, 2017, https://www.youtube.com/
    watch?v=Oil5wIcwJN4&feature=youtu.be

PHOTOS IN MULTIPLE DIGITAL REPOSITORIES

"The Bancroft Library Presents The 1906 San Francisco Earthquake and Fire."
    Bancroft Library, University of California, Berkeley http://bancroft.berkeley.
    edu/collections/earthquakeandfire/index2.html
Online Catalog, California Historical Society http://207.67.203.81/C95040/
    OPAC/Search/SimpleSearch.aspx
Picture Catalog, California State Library http://catalog.library.
    ca.gov/F/?func=find-e-0&local_base=images
Chinese Historical Society of America – History Pin project http://www.chsa.
    org/2011/04/20/history-pin/
Prints and Photographs, Online Catalog – Library of Congress http://www.loc.
    gov/pictures/
The San Francisco Historical Photograph Collection, San Francisco Public
    Library, http://sfpl.org/index.php?pg=0200000301

ABOUT THE AUTHOR

(Tandemvines Media)

Denise E. Clifton is the founder of Tandemvines Media, a multimedia company that works with organizations and authors to create stories that are multidimensional experiences. She is committed to crafting narratives that encourage readers to explore – through reading, watching videos, making a new recipe or visiting a new place.

Denise writes about food history and is especially drawn to stories that teach about the evolution of a place through its food. She is passionate about using these compelling tales to help others connect to these special locales. While researching the restaurants featured in *Tables From The Rubble*, she learned about San Francisco's Italian and Chinese immigrants, neighborhood development, the boxing world, and Prohibition history. She also explored the unique challenges faced by families whose businesses span generations – as well as the stories behind different types of focaccia, raw-fish salad, Green Goddess salad dressing and bloater toast.

Oh, and she ate very well – though she admits she hasn't tried the bloater toast. Yet.

Denise worked as a designer, editor, art director, and department head for 20 years at the *Seattle Times*. She has been recognized with multiple awards for her design, and provided art direction and project management for two Pulitzer Prize-winning teams. Denise was a Stanford University Knight Fellow in 2004-05.

In 2012, Denise formed Tandemvines Media with her husband, Christopher Cellars. *Tables From The Rubble* was the first multimedia book release from Tandemvines, which is based in Seattle, Wash. Tandemvines has since produced several multimedia and print books, including *An Air That Still Kills*, which was honored as the 2016 iBook of the Year. For more on Tandemvines, see www.tandemvines.com. Email Denise at denise@tandemvines.com

ABOUT THE MULTIMEDIA EDITION

Tables From The Rubble is also available in a visually rich multimedia edition designed for MacOS and iOS. The enhanced edition offers colorful visual storytelling impossible to render in the print edition, including:

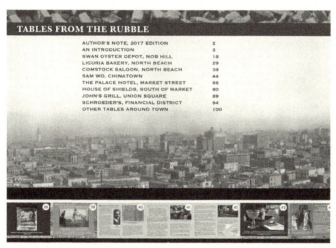

- An interactive map showing the burn zone and where the featured restaurants opened after the earthquake
- Several videos featuring the modern restaurants
- A gallery of menus from the Palace Hotel going back more than a century. The menu images can be enlarged for easier reading
- Several early-twentieth century newspaper pages, which can be enlarged
- Audio of "On San Francisco Bay," a song recorded by Billy Murray in 1907
- Many additional historic and modern photographs

For the multimedia edition for MacOS and iOS, go to the book's page online at bit.ly/tablerubble.

For a Kindle edition of this book, go to amazon.com. The Kindle edition does not include multimedia.

Made in the USA
Las Vegas, NV
05 February 2021